FIFTH EDITION

THE MODERN YUCATAN DICTIONARY

RALF HOLLMANN

ILLUSTRATIONS BY GREENWOOD

HAMACA PRESS

Copyright © 2013 Ralf Hollmann

All Rights Reserved. No part of this publication may be copied, sold, used, or reproduced in any form without prior written permission from the copyright holder.

Book design: Lee Steele
Illustrations: Greenwood
Cover photo: Lonely Planet Images

Published by Hamaca Press
Fairfield, Connecticut, USA., and Mérida, Yucatán, Mexico
www.hamacapress.com

ISBN: 978-0-9884337-5-5

Library of Congress Control Number: 2013942077

INTRODUCTION

Part of the fun of moving somewhere new is of course, the language, and the Yucatan peninsula in southern Mexico is no exception, what with all those old Spanish words no longer used in other parts of the Spanish-speaking world mixed in with Mayan terminology and grammar.

The Mayans, you see, were the original inhabitants of this part of the world and were doing just fine thank you until the Spanish arrived, when they became the only indigenous group never fully conquered by those ambitious, gold-digging conquistadores, and their stubborn resistance is visible even today; in many of Yucatan's rural communities you will hear Mayan spoken without a trace of Spanish, and in the cities, Mayan terms are used alongside Spanish by all socio-economic classes.

The little book in your hot little hands is a living, breathing thing; it has been several years in the making and is the product of continuous listening and annotating by its author, a Canadian who has lived in the Yucatan for over 25 years. This is the fifth revision of this informative dictionary, featuring an ever-increasing collection of unique, entertaining, and occasionally rude terminology unique to the area.

This evolving work includes Mayan, Spanish, and slang, as well as local words and expressions whose definitions are not ordinarily found elsewhere, all presented in what is hopefully an informative as well as entertaining writing style. This book does not yet hope to be the definitive Spanish or even Mayan dictionary, but rather a collection of terms you will hear, explained in their local context. If you are new to Merida and/or visiting our formerly "White City," you will find these helpful.

If you speak Spanish and would like more information on how and why Yucatecans speak the way they do, visit the UADY (Universidad Autónoma de Yucatán) bookstore and ask for a recording (on my last visit there it was still available on cassette—yes, cassette) of local poet and writer Fernando Espejo's "El Habla del Yucateco," a conference given on the subject. It is very entertaining and will give you greater insight into the Spanish spoken in the Yucatan.

(And don't hesitate to let me know your thoughts on this small literary effort. You can write me at ralf.hollmann@gmail.com)

About the author

Ralf Hollmann is a Canadian freelance writer and travel consultant living in Mexico's Yucatan peninsula for over 25 years. One of Merida's first bloggers, Ralf has also written for *Yucatan Today* and *Yucatan Living* and is a TripAdvisor Destination Expert on the area.

Ralf's passion for language has led him not only to write, but to create the Mayan Xic line of clothing and souvenirs, dedicated to the preservation and promotion of this peculiar blend of Spanish, with its Mayan and colonial-era influences, spoken in the Yucatan and unique to the Spanish-speaking world.

About the illustrator

Douglas Greenwood, called "Greenwood" by his friends, *Madera Verde* by amigos, and *Yax Che* in Maya, grew up in Florida and studied at Ft. Lauderdale Art Institute and Jacksonville University. With a portfolio including 1,000-square-foot murals, editorial cartoons, and book illustrations, his impressionistic style varies but is always uplifting.

Greenwood and his wife, Cherie, have lived happily in Merida since 2007 with their wonder dog, Buddy Love, and the Maya ruin jungle princess kitty rescue, Maya. Greenwood's illustrations also appear in *Our Yucatan*, published by Hamaca Press.

DEDICATED TO MARU

Every book should be dedicated to someone, even a humble dictionary like this one, which probably falls outside the normal or official definition of the term. And so, I would like to dedicate this book to my dear wife, Maru, who has lovingly prodded and pushed me to publish my neurotic attempts at writing and online ramblings, in the form of a book. This is a first step in that direction.

Thank you for your unconditional support, faith, and patience!

A

a *(ah)*—The first letter of the alphabet; but, in Yucatan, if you say it right, it is a Mayan term of affirmation, not only of what someone says to you, but what you are saying yourself. The tone starts in the middle of your vocal range and goes down as you say *aaaaaaaahhhhhhhh*.

When someone is talking to you, you can show (or fake) interest by interjecting a heartfelt aaaaahhhh every once in a while. If the person you are talking to is Yucatecan, he or she, in most cases and unless overdone, will understand that you are paying attention; if the person you are *aaaaah*-ing is not from the Yucatan, he or she may think you are making fun of them and may become hostile.

If you are the one doing the talking, take a cue from the speaking habits of some of the older people from the pueblos in rural Yucatan and don't let anyone interrupt your monologue. Fill in the space between your words and sentences with your own aaaahhhhs.

▶▶ *Entonces, empezó a llover y me metí . . . aaahhhhhhh . . . y me dice la suegra así me dice 'qué haces aquí que no ves que somos MUCHOS' y le digo ah sí, ta bueno, quieres que me agarre la lluvia . . . aaaaaaahhhhhh . . . etc. etc.*

The letter *a* is also a unique form of turning any verb into future tense. I have not heard anyone in the Yucatan ever say *comeré más tarde* (I will eat later); it's always *a cómo después*. In his conference on Yucatecan speech (available on tape—yes, cassette tape—at the local UADY bookstore) Fernando Espejo explains this and gives the following beautiful, concise, example:

▶▶ *A te mueres, a lloro.*
Should you die, I will cry.

acostumbrar *(ah-cost-oom-BRAHR)* VERB—What happens to your *muchacha* (SEE *muchacha*) after she has been in your employ for a while. It literally means "to get used to" but here it's used to denote a general contentment and reasonable satisfaction with a job.

▸▸ *¿Por qué sigues trabajando con Don Juan?*
Why are you still working for Mr. Juan?

▸▸ *Es que ya me acostumbré.*
I like it/I'm too lazy to look for something better/it's an OK job.

agarrar (*ah-gah-RAHR*)—To grab a hold of something; as in ¡*agárralos, son gratis!* (grab 'em they're free!), often heard when someone is hesitant to take something from someone who's offering; the third party usually makes this statement.

▸▸ *¡Agarra el centro de mesa, para eso los ponen!*
Take the flower arrangement from the table (at a reception or dinner), that's what they are for!

Other examples include:

▸▸ *Agarra tu cambio.*
There's your change, take it.

▸▸ *Me estaba agarrando.*
He was feeling me up.

▸▸ *Me estaba agarroteando.*
He was really feeling me up.

There are more applications for this handy little verb, but my personal favourite is its versatility in traffic situations, where it is used instead of the probably more correct *tomar*. (SEE *tomar*)

▸▸ *Voy a agarrar carretera.*
I'm going to take the highway.

▸▸ *Agarras la 20.*
Take 20th street. (When getting directions.)

ahuech (*ah-WETCH*) A STRONG AFFIRMATIVE EXCLAMATION—This is a contraction and polite(r) form of saying *a huevo* or where *huevo* is understood to refer to testicles, so you see it's not the most graceful thing to say on a first date or when meeting the inlaws for the first time. This is used when answering a statement that someone has made to you that is definitely true, most certainly. E.g. *¿Vamos a la disco?* Are we going to the disco? (These are your friends asking, not your date). ¡*Ahuech!*, you pronounce firmly, thus demonstrating your knowledge of the local (sub) culture.

albañil (*al-bah-NYEEL*)—Probably the lowest rung in the Yucatecan career ladder. In effect, a brick layer or construction worker. These poor (as in financially challenged) people travel in rag-tag packs and the vehicle of choice (they themselves have none) is the *camión de redilas* (a pickup with a box on the back, driven by the *ingeniero de la obra* or supervising engineer) where they travel standing-room-only along Yucatan's highways and byways. Highlights of their trips to and from their constantly changing places of employment include:

» the inevitable pulling over of the vehicle by our always vigilant state and federal police, where the *ingeniero* or whoever is driving must fork over some cash to be able to continue this illegal, but in most cases only, available form of public transportation;

» seeing a person of the female sex walking along the side of the road, whereupon the entire standing population of the back of the truck will twist and turn their heads to get a glimpse of said female, whistle, and point, as if they had never seen a woman before, or perhaps to make eye contact and thereby initiate a charming love story.

alisar (*ah-lee-SAHR*)—To smooth over or out. In homes where the iron was reserved for more proper clothing, t-shirts and the like were simply washed, dried, and smoothed out to remove the most blatant and outstanding wrinkles. The term persists and many rural ladies, working for the ladies that can't or don't want to even think about their housework, refer to the ironing of the clothes as *alisar*, not *planchar*. (SEE ALSO *Saga*)

Americano (*you know how to pronounce this one*) 1) person or thing from the U.S.

2) Person or thing from North Central or South America. The actual definition of this word is tricky. If you use it in a conversation or someone refers to you as one and you're from the U.S., and nobody gets upset, then you're alright. But if you run into one of those left wing Communist idealists or PRD people and you call yourself an *Americano*, look out 'cuz you'll get an earful on ugly Yankee imperialism and how everyone from both North and South America is an American, not just those usurpers from the U.S. of A. Even Canadians. So take THAT.

3) Regular black coffee is called *café americano* or simply *americano*.

amigo (*ah-MEE-goh*) FRIENDLY NOUN—That infuriatingly common salutation reserved for us foreigners when approached by someone selling something. A local of a certain age will be called *caballero*, or even *señor*, but upon seeing a paleface, the salesperson immediately goes into his or her "Mexico, the *amigo* country" mode, and offers us the pitch. Upon hearing *hola amigo* immediately know that you are going to get a sales pitch. For example:

> ▸ *¡Amigo! ¡Hamacas!*
> Do they really think that every damn gringo look-a-like wants a hammock?

> ▸ *¿Ya tiene Eskai, amigo?* (SEE *Eskai*)
> No, I don't want *ESS-sky*.

> ▸ *Hola amigo.*
> Anyone who calls me friend from the initial contact is definitely not my friend.

animal (*ah-nih-MAHL*) NOUN—If you are behaving abominably or in such a way as to cause others to seriously doubt your intellectual capacity, you are *un animal*. Driving in Merida, you will encounter many specimens that fit into the animal category, in which also resides many a politician.

anolar (*ah-noh-LAHR*) VERB—The first time I heard this word I was dumbstruck. I had heard that *anolar* roughly translates as "to suck on," as in a hard candy, but it is an old Spanish word and I had never actually heard it in real life. Standing in a store one day, a lady took a candy from a jar on the counter and asked me, "*¿Se anolam?*" I don't know if she thought I would say no, you chew them; in any case it was the first time I heard it—it is very possible that you will never come across it in conversations with anyone under the age of 30 these days. One of my faithful online readers, writing from Scotland of all places (!), told me to check on the Mayan origins of this word since she had lived in Merida and was pretty sure that was where it came from—sure enough, consulting my trusty Cordemex special edition Mayan dictionary, the word comes from the Mayan *nol*, which means to roll around in the mouth, as in a small seeded fruit like the guaya/huaya for example. So it's an españolizacion of the original Mayan *nol*. Exciting stuff, this language business....

apoltronado (*ah-pohl-troh-NAH-doe*) STATE OF LETHARGIC INACTIVITY—When you see someone sitting in a chair, slouching even, rolls of midsection hanging over their belt, their expression lifeless in a state of semi-consciousness (perhaps they have just had a big meal and are in the digestion process) they can be said to be *apoltronado*.

apesgar (*ah-pez-GAHR*) VERB—Meaning to press, as in a button on a piece of electronic equipment or a casino slot machine. This is another old Spanish word, still in use today in the Yucatan. One of my favorite memories involving this word was while trying to get a Mayan *muchacha* to turn off the computer via telephone during a thunderstorm. During the conversation, I asked her to find the escape key on the keyboard and when she did she asked me "*¿lo apesgo?*" which took me completely by surprise since I hadn't heard the word before.

armado (*ahr-MAH-doe*) ADVERB—Armed, as in armed with a knife or pistol. But in Yucatecan society, this verb is applied when you are ascertaining whether or not the fellow next to you has a drink. The scenario is as follows: You get up to fix yourself a drink at the table where the host has set up bottles of vodka, rum, whisky, Coke, and Diet Coke and under which an ice chest filled with bags of ice is located, from which you scoop ice into your glass with your hands. As you pour Coke over your rum you turn to your buddy (in this case your *compadre*) and ask "*¿Tas armado, compadre?*" to which he may or may not nod in affirmation, holding his drink up for you to see that he is, indeed, *armado*.

aquello (*ah-KAY-yoh*) NOUN—Although in its regular form the word means "that," in certain social circles "that" refers to . . . sexual intercourse. I have heard of women, who can be totally frank and open about such things, discuss their sex lives in a roundabout way with friends:

▸▸ *En medio del huracán, él me pidió aquello.*
In the middle of the hurricane, he asked for "that."

aquellito (*ah-kay-EE-toh*)—The shortened version of *aquello*, can and is often used as *aquello*, above, or also to refer to a body part that is either embarrassing or unmentionable for some other reason.

▸▸ *¿Te lavaste aquellito?*
Did you wash "that"?
. . . is a perfectly understandable question when put to a child.

asu (*ah-suh*) EXCLAMATION—This is not Yucatecan, but again, something you might hear on the street from someone who does not look like a *Yuca*. It is a term from the nearby state of Tabasco (no, there is no Tabasco sauce in Tabasco) whose inhabitants have many choice expressions that could be the subject of another dictionary like this one. You will hear it used much like the local favourite *uay* as an expression of fear or surprise.

awech (*ah-wetch*)—(SEE *ahuech*, above)

a westinjaus (*ah-westinghouse*)—This is another slang-y, street version of the expression *awech* or *ahuech* above.

avenida (*ah-veh-NEE-duh*) NOUN—Literally translated as avenue. *Avenida* can be any main street. In the exciting and glamorous world of Yucatecan real estate, having a house *en la avenida* is desirable. Having a house *en esquina*—with street frontage on two sides, is highly desirable, although for the life of me I can't understand why, unless you have the cunning plan of renting your home out as a business at some future date.

B

b (*beh*)—The second letter of the alphabet. Nothing special about it, except that in Mexico and other parts of Latin America it is often confused with the *v*, making it a very versatile letter indeed.

▸▸ *Bery bersatile.*

This makes correct spelling (and pronunciation) a real challenge not only in the Yucatan, but throughout all of Mexico. When spelling, people may ask you *¿b alta o b chica?* (upper or lower b?) so they know if they should put a *b* or a *v*. One Yucatecan boss I had used to say "*bamos al var.*" Mexican pop idol Luis Miguel, on his Romance album where he mutilates traditional romantic Mexican music as only he can, sings *Vésame (Besame Mucho)* quite clearly and irritatingly. Even more hair-raising was an 'N Sync wannabe group from Venezuela called Uff, and their stomach-turning hit *Vy Vy* (Bye Bye), *Arrividerci mi Amor*. And during the George W. Bush tirade against Iraq, a local radio announcer called the capital city of that oil-rich nation *VagDad*. Some other examples you may encounter:

▸▸ *bienbenidos*
welcome

▸▸ *belador*
caretaker

▸▸ *bamos*
let's go

bah

bah (*BAH*) EXPRESSION—Whenever someone tells you something that surprises you, you can exclaim ¡*bah!* to indicate you are listening and you are surprised.

barbaridad (*BAR-bari-DAHD*) NOUN—A barbarity. Something barbaric. Used if something that has happened or been done is beyond belief; incredible. For example:

>> *Es una barbaridad que haya tantos extranjeros en Mérida.*
It's incredible that there are so many foreigners in Merida.

bárbaro (*BAHR-bah-roh*) ADJECTIVE—Barbarian, usually used when something or someone is, or has done something, unbelievable.

>> *¡Qué bárbaro!*
That's incredible!

barrida (*bah-REE-duh*) NOUN—Literally, a sweep; what insecure teenage girls do to each other in the mall. The *barrida* is a quick sweep or scan of a possible competitor's hair, makeup, and outfit and goes from hair colour to shoes in a moment to determine social status and acceptability of the subject in an instant. Very important at the class and self-conscious pre- and early-teenage level. Thanks to my daughter for this bit of enlightenment.

basura (*bah-SUE-rah*) NOUN—Usually referring to garbage, waste, etc., this word has a special meaning in Yucatan in that it includes leaves from trees. A great part of the resistance many Yucatecans have to maintaining trees on their properties comes from the fact that, as they will invariably argue when you confront them on the casualness with which they will cut down a perfectly healthy and beautiful tree, it produces too much "garbage." Television programs and modern music can also be described as *basura* by folks of a certain age.

bicho (*BEE-cho*) NOUN—**1)** Any kind of insect or bug.

>> *Mira el tamaño de ese bicho.*
Look at the size of that bug

bicho

2) A common nickname for anyone called Victor. Yucatecans are famous for inventing nicknames that last a lifetime, and this is not an unusual specimen; e.g. *El Bicho Milke* (Victor Milke); **3)** A strange person. *Ese Manolo es un bicho raro*—meaning that Manolo is kind of weird; the way he dresses, acts, or looks falls outside the standards of "normality" for most Yucatecans. Rarely used for women.

blanquillo (*blahn-KEE-oh*) NOUN—From the word *blanco*, or white. People from the pueblos and rural areas use this term a lot, substituting it for the correct *huevos*, which again has sexual connotations (SEE *ahuech*, *hueva*) and it perhaps didn't sound nice in the prudish days of long skirts and haciendas; the term remains in use to this day. *¿Tiene blanquillos?* is certainly easier to answer with a straight face than *¿Tiene huevos?*

bobox (*boh-BOSH*) BODY PART NOUN—The Mayan word for tailbone, this word is also applied (SEE *pirix*) to the general area where the tailbone is located. A common complaint of the elderly is "*me duele el bobox*" ("ouch, my tailbone") usually said with a grimace when they get up from that semi-comfortable chair on the sidewalk when it's time to go to bed.

Bostom's (*BOSS-tohms*) NAME—This is how Yucatecans call a popular Canadian pizza franchise, opened a few years ago in Merida. Now with two locations! Once someone said: "*Vamos a comer a Jiustom*," getting their Boston and Houston just a little mixed up.

bota (*BOH-tah*) VERB—If you throw something away, *lo botas*. Usually this refers to garbage. NOUN—A boot. Former Mexican president Vicente Fox made them famous during his six-year term in office at Los Pinos. In Merida, *bota* can also mean "vote" as in "*Bota por el PAM*" (SEE *PAM*), since the letter *b* and *v* are completely interchangeable in Merida and other parts of Mexico as well, probably, thanks to a quality Spanish curriculum that also mixes up soft *c*'s, *z*'s, and *s*'s.

boxito (*boh-SHEE-toh*) LOCAL TERM OF ENDEARMENT—What Yucatecans, male and female, call each other. Calling someone *boxito lindo*, or *boxita linda* for the girls, is not uncommon today. *Box* is Mayan and means "black;" the *ito* part is a Spanish suffix to indicate the diminutive. Wow, that was technical. Remember the *x* is pronounced *sh* or you will give yourself away as a non-Yucatecan!

brackets (*you know how to pronounce this one*) NOUN—The local term for braces (think teeth).

>> *A Seidy le pusieron brackets.*
Seidy's got braces.

brackets

buenas (*BWAY-nuss* if there are people; *bway-NAAASS* if there is no one there, e.g. a front gate)—The accepted greeting, spoken loudly and at no one in particular, upon entering a crowded room or doctors waiting area; a shortened version of *buenas tardes* or *buenos días*. If the house you are visiting belongs to someone you don't know, you will stand at the metal gate and shout ¡BUENAAAS! *(SEE ALSO* pronunciation above) with the second syllable accented and about a fifth of an octave higher than the first syllable until someone gets tired of your melodious voice and comes to the door to see what you want. Particularly useful if you are selling door to door or trying the "Hi, can I have a glass of water?" scam to case a house for future goods extraction.

bueno (*BWAY-no*) 1) ADJECTIVE—Most visitors from the U.S., Canada, and places further away already know this one; it means "good." But here in the land of the deer and the pheasant, *bueno* has another, more significant meaning to all those Yucatecans in love with their wallets and bank accounts.

Let me explain.

One day you might be asked, while on the subject of favourite restaurants or good place to eat "typical" food: *"¿Ya probaste el queso relleno en Chapur? ¡Esta re-bueno!"* (Have you tried the stuffed cheese in Chapur? It's really good!) This does not necessarily mean that the food is that great; rather it means that it's really cheap! Certain Yucatecans are very conscious of the money that they spend and do not want to let anyone take advantage of them. So if they feel that they are getting a good deal, this is much more important than the actual quality of what it is that they're purchasing. Among some locals, there is a feeling of satisfaction in knowing that you paid the lowest possible price for something; rather than getting screwed by the merchant, I managed to screw him, ha ha.

So if someone tells you that such and such is really *bueno*, take this definition into consideration, since your idea of what is good may not precisely coincide!

2) The word also can be used as a sexual reference.

▸ *El marido de Fulana está rebueno (the re prefix is emphatic).*
Fulanas' husband is really hot.

This is also available for use in the female context, as in

▸ *Esa Niurka está buenísima.*
That Niurka is so hot.

In Yucatecan circles Niurka would be Niurka Marcos, former sexy Cuban dancer turned television star thanks to some creative marriage tactics, *(SEE Cuba)* who got her start on the star-studded local stations.

Do not answer *estoy bueno* if someone asks how you are, as this answer means you are good in bed, unless of course that is what you want to say. The correct answer is *estoy bien*.

3) GREETING AND FAREWELL—*Bueno* is also what you say when picking up a ringing telephone; the first syllable *BWAY* is a higher note than the second one *NO*, especially if you want to sound like you studied at the Colegio Merida. Equally useful as a farewell, both on the phone and in person when leaving a party or ending a casual encounter at the *tortillería* in the *mercado*. Yucatecans are famous for their repeated *buenos* to each other when saying good night.

bueno pués (*BWAY-no-PWESS*)—This is a very necessary phrase to be used by anyone aspiring to be a DJ on Yucatecan radio. It must be uttered approximately every four or five words, between all songs and all commercials and in all lame interviews with local pseudo-celebrities. This phrase will make you want to rip out your radio and throw it through the windows of your car, if you are in the least bit as neurotic as the author of this book.

bulto (*BOOL-toh*) NOUN—A large package, wrapped in twine ready to be shipped somewhere, as in henequén, or plastic bags. In modern-day Merida, *bulto* is also used to describe anything that you carry that has your stuff, or *chucherías* *(SEE chucherías)* in it. Thus, the elegant Gucci handbag you are carrying is referred to by your *muchacha* or even someone of higher education but untravelled, unglamorously as your *bulto*.

Burger King (*boor-gehr-KIM*)—Again, no definition required, but note the pronunciation and syllabic emphasis. While McDonald's opens a new store every 17 minutes somewhere in the world, Burger King had to close over 200 locations during dour economic times. But locals prefer the Whopper (often pronounced *Whooper*) over the Big Mac.

buscar (*boo-SCAHR*)—This great verb, meaning "to look for" (in Castilian Spanish) and also "to find" (in the Yucatan) has been an endless source of amusement for those who arrive in Merida from other parts of the country and have not been blessed with a Mayan cultural legacy. According to linguists and experts on the subject, the Mayas used one verb for "to look for" and that was it. If they found it; well, they had finished looking for it. The usual conversation goes like this:

▸▸ *¿Ya buscastes el martillo?*
Have you found the hammer?

▸▸ *No, todavía no lo busco.*
No I still haven't found it.

▸▸ *Sí, ya lo busqué.*
Yeah, I've found it.

The joke that all the outsiders like to laugh at is:

▸▸ *Busco, busco, y no lo busco.*
I look, I look, and I can't find it.

▸▸ Another use of the word: If you are looking for someone like a new employee or something like your lost dog, you might start a poster with the words *SE BUSCA* which is roughly the same idea as "lost" (in the case of the dog) or "wanted" (in the case of the employee or a criminal).

C

c (*seh*)—Third letter of the alphabet. Like the letters *b* and *v*, this letter sounds like the *s* and the *z*, leading to more confusion when it comes to spelling. The funniest example of this confusion was painted on a wall in giant letters in a little *pueblito* during Patricio Patron's campaign for a seat in the Yucatecan Senate. Instead of *Patricio—Senador*, they had painted *Patricio—Cenador*, as in the guy everyone wants to have over for *la cena* (dinner).

cabrón (*cah-BRONE*) 1) NOUN—This is a "bad" word that is becoming more and more common, especially among the younger set, which seems to use it every two words in a conversation. Not to be used in mixed company; however, you will hear it more and more in the most public of places, including a recent exchange in the supermarket between a supervisor and an employee in the fruits and vegetables department.

▶▶ *Ven a limpiar esto, cabrón.*
Come and clean this up, motherf**ker.

2) ADJECTIVE—This word can also be used to describe something that is highly unlikely to occur or extremely difficult. If you are going through a difficult moment in your business, for example, and someone asks how things are going, you might reply "*maare* (SEE *mare*), *'ta cabrón*" referring to the situation. Again, not to be used in mixed company.

▶▶ *¿Vas a Progreso el sábado?*
Are you going to Progreso on Saturday?

▶▶ *No, 'ta cabrón.*
No, it's highly unlikely.

(SEE ALSO *encabronado*)

cachucha (*kah-CHOO-chah*) NOUN—This little gem is a hat. As in a baseball cap. While in other parts of the country it known as a *gorra*, in Yucatan it always a

cachucha

THE MODERN YUCATAN DICTIONARY   **19**

cachucha. There is even a local business that devotes itself entirely to the sale of caps and is known, duh, as Mr. Cachuchas. The sound of this word is much more fun to pronounce than the more difficult (double *r*) *gorra*.

café (*cah-FEH*) NOUN—Merida is finally coming around to drinking real coffee. In the old days, when yours truly first came to live here, ordering a coffee resulted in a cup of hot water being set before you, along with a container of Nescafé and a spoon. Ordering *café con leche* produced the same results, with hot milk (powdered Nido) replacing the hot water. In many parts of the Yucatan, where the very idea of a double decaf *espresso* or a *frappuccino* is the equivalent of seeing a flying saucer land on the local *henequén* plantation, this abominable practice continues.

café

cagar (*kah-GAHR*) VERB—A truly versatile word!

1) Literally, and vulgarly speaking, to shit, defecate, etc. Don't use this at the Club Campestre if you're invited and trying to make a good impression when visiting the men's (or ladies) room.

2) To screw up in a major way.

   Why is it versatile you ask? Let me present you with some examples:

   ▸ *Me estoy cagando.*
   Very vulgar way to express your imminent urge to celebrate a bowel movement.

   ▸ *La está cagando*
   This doesn't mean the same as the first in the third person; rather, it means "he's screwing up."

   ▸ *Está igualito—parece que lo cagó su papá.*
   This expression is used when an offspring resembles almost exactly his or her father, not only in physical appearance, but in most other ways as well.

   ▸ *Me caga que me haga eso.*
   I just hate it so much when she does that. (Thanks to my daughter for this one.)

   ▸ *Me estoy cagando de miedo.*
   I am filling my trousers with fearful anticipation.

cajera (*cah-HAIR-ah*) NOUN—1) Cashier, female.

2) A type of wrinkly orange with a bitter flavour, not commonly found in the produce section of Publix or Safeway and increasingly rare even in local supermarkets.

cajero (*cah-HAIR-oh*) NOUN—1) Cashier, male.

2) The machine the folks in the U.S. call the A.T.M. that spits out cash.

caliente (*cali-YEN-teh*) ADJECTIVE—Hot. Someone ordering a soup might complain to the waiter that it is *caliente*. Duh. But in Merida, things are never that hot; coffee, soups, and so on are served almost hot, or very warm. Please do not make the classic newcomer to the Spanish language mistake of proclaiming yourself as *caliente* when you are feeling the tropical heat! This means that you are hot, as in horny, and some people might see that as an invitation or at the very least an excess of familiarity (too much information, stop!).

camino blanco (*cah-MEE-noh BLAHN-coh*) WHITE NOUN—Literally translated as "white road," the term refers to any road that is not paved. Many roads to smaller rural areas or a spectacular *cenote* or Mayan ruin in the Yucatan are still unpaved, rocky, bump-fests that will test the mettle of your metal (think shock absorbers, oil pan, mufflers, and the like). Since the crushed stone sprinkled occasionally is made of our local limestone and is white, this is probably where the term comes from.

ca'on (*cah-OWN*) NOUN and ADJECTIVE—This is a shortened version of the word *cabrón* discussed earlier, where the *b* and *r* have been eliminated. Very popular as of this writing, again, among younger people, but used by anyone in the mid-teens to late-forties age bracket. Thanks to my daughter for this.

carretera (*cah-reh-TEH-rah*) DRIVING NOUN—*Carretera* means highway. Sometimes when you are speaking to a person of little education, often in a small village, any paved road, no matter how NOT a highway it is, will be referred to as *la carretera*. This is a double R word which means you will have to roll those double *r*'s (but not the second *r*) on the front of your tongue, I'm afraid. Good luck.

casino (*cah-SEE-noh*) NOUN—A gambling joint. These were non-existent until the end of the Vicente Fox administration, when Santiago Creel, in effect the vice-president, signed an order allowing the establishment of casinos in Mexico, presumably—one can speculate—in exchange for a jackpot of his own. You can now find casinos in most malls in Merida and the younger generation is horrified to discover that Mamá and Papá are gamblin away their inheritances there.

cenote (*seh-NOH-teh*) HOLE-IN-THE-GROUND NOUN—*Cenotes* are holes and caves in the surface of the Yucatan where you can access the water table. The crystal clear blue waters have become something of a tourist attraction but I suspect that at some point, when water contamination becomes a serious concern, access to these natural swimming holes will become more controlled and perhaps even restricted.

The word *cenote* comes from a mangling (nothing new here) by the early Spanish settlers of the Mayan word *dzonot*. Many place names in the Yucatan end with the word *dzonot*, which usually means that there is a *cenote* in the area. (SEE *dzonot*)

centro (*SEN-troh*) NOUN—The middle of something. In Merida, it invariably means downtown; people from the upscale northern part of the city lament that to buy their pampered children's school festival costumes or accessories, they must drive *hasta el centro*, usually accompanied by a rolling of the eyes and a voice filled with weariness and resignation, answered with a sympathetic shaking of the head by the listener who understands what that implies. If you are taking a bus anywhere in this formerly "White City," the routes are designed in such a way that you must always go to *el centro*, where you will find your connecting bus. *El centro* is synonymous with noise, traffic, heat, smog, and great masses of the other half of Merida's population, who shop and work there. Prices are always cheaper downtown, which explains why Merida's *clase acomodada*, always on the lookout for the cheapest possible bargain, must make the sacrificial journey and thereby be subjected to the unpleasant reality of the "other Merida."

In an interesting language-related aside; among the local expat (i.e. gringo) population, it is not uncommon to hear them say that they live in *centro* as thought it were the name of a suburb or something instead of *el centro* which would be what the locals call it.

CFE —The initials for the national power company monopoly, the Comision Federal de Electricidad, a monument to bureaucracy combined with a bloated union strangulating and castrating business and homeowners throughout the country with outrageous rates and spotty service. They are against privatization, but the company should be sold—and soon—to anyone; it can only get better. I suggest immediate privatization and breaking it up into smaller parts; then it might become more efficient. (SEE *Comision, La*)

chafa (*CHAH-fah*) POORLY MADE ADJECTIVE—1) When something is poorly put together, a piece of equipment doesn't work or a plan doesn't gel; the moment calls for an exclamation of *¡qué chafa!*

2) If there is a contest and a winner announced, inevitably there will be one or more Yucatecans who will feel like they didn't get a proper chance to respond or participate and that the whole game was rigged. They will then cry "*¡es chafa!*" which in English would be "not fair!"

chalan (*chuh-LAHN*) NOUN—This is the guy who every *ingenierio* or other professional male has accompanying him in his daily work. If you need to measure something, you pass the measuring tape to the *chalan* who will do the necessary bending and stretching to get those measurements to you. You are moving something from point A to B? You have the *chalan* load up the pickup and then drive him (preferably he is in the back trying to keep his balance and hold something down at the same time) to the destination, park, light a cigarette, and wait for the *chalan* to unload everything. The *chalan* is the workplace equivalent of the domestic and housebound *mozo*. (SEE *mozo*)

chamba (*CHAHM-bah*)—Work: if you have it, *tienes chamba*. If you are working, *estás chambeando*. If you work really hard, you would be called *chambeador*. If something is not working, *no chambea*.

chaperón (*chah-per-ROHN*) NOUN—A rapidly disappearing tradition in Yucatecan dating life, this is the term applied to the little brother or sister who must accompany a young girl and her date to watch the couple and report back to the parents (of the girl, mostly) of any transgressions on the part of their possibly overactive hormones that might result in shame and humiliation for the family. The *chaperón* can be bought off, however, by sending him or her with some pesos to get him or herself an ice cream, candy, or whatever, thereby providing an opening for an intimate, albeit all-too-short, exchange of affections between the couple.

chaya (*CHYE-yah*) NOUN/ADJECTIVE—A spinach-like leafy vegetable, supposedly full of nutritive qualities and traditionally used by Mayans for food and medicinal purposes. Try the *agua de chaya* next time you visit La Susana Internacional restaurant in Kanasin. Thanks to our intrepid and previously alluded-to reader, based in Scotland at the moment, who reminds me that *chaya* also refers to something cheesy or corny. If you found something (or someone) to be definitely below par, you would say:

chaya

>> *¡Qué chaya!*
How corny!

>> *Está chayísimo.*
It's really corny.

chel (*CHEL*) NOUN—The Mayan term for those of you who are fair-skinned and or fair-haired.

>> *¡Qué onda, chel!*
What's up, blondie!

chela (*CHE-lah*) NOUN—The female version of the *chel*, above. Also, a *chela* is a beer, plural *chelas*. You can substitute *chelas* for *chevas*.

>> *Unas chelas bien heladas*
A couple of cold ones

chekenyim (*CHECK-en-yim*) LIT NOUN—That light on the dash of your car that indicates a problem with your motor. Your mechanic might ask:

>> *¿'Ta prendido el checkenyim?*
Is the Check Engine light on?

cheva (*CHE-vah*) NOUN—Another popular term for beer. Singular *cheva*, plural *chevas*. Uses include:

>> *Vamos por las chevas.*
Let's go get some beers.

>> *¿Nos tomamos unas chevas?*
Wanna go drink some beers?

>> *¿Y las chevas?*
And the beer? (*as in* where is it?)

cheva

▸▸ *Te invito (a) una cheva.*
I'll buy you a beer.

Chichén Itzá (*chee-CHEN eet-ZAH*) MAYAN SITE—After adding Uxmal (SEE *Uxmal*), I figured *Chichen* (as we call it around these parts) should get a mention as well. Arguably the most famous Mayan site, *Chichén Itzá* is now a New World Wonder and everyone and their *perro* comes to see it, especially from Cancun, about two hours away. If you must visit, remember that everything is roped off; you cannot walk behind or around a building, let alone dream of actually climbing or touching one. There are pesky vendors hawking trinkets and hovering around like persistent horseflies with phrases like "good price for you my friend" and "cheaper than Walmart." A good time to avoid both the crushing crowds and vexing vendors is as soon as the site opens at 8 a.m.

chile (*CHEE-leh*) NOUN—Everyone knows what a *chile* is: hot little peppers! In the Yucatan there is really only one that captures the imagination, the ultra-hot habanero. If you are like many a Yucatecan, you will always accompany your meals with *chile*. *Chile* means habanero, cut up and served on a little plate, often with lime juice and salt.

chile

Some just take bites of a habanero *chile* between mouthfuls of whatever the meal happens to be.

Many Yucatecans cannot (or will not) eat a meal without their *chile*; it is of no importance whether they are in Italy having osso bucco or in Hong Kong eating lacquered duck. He or she will call the waiter over and ask for *chile*. The waiter will likely not understand and so the Yucatecan will again say "*chile*" in a slightly louder voice while at the same time making a vertical cutting motion with the right hand on the horizontally outstretched left hand, as if cutting an imaginary *chile,* thus providing the visual stimulus that would convey the appropriate message to the waiter. As a result of many Yucatecans' failure to communicate in this fashion over the years (and coming back to complain about it), it is not at all unusual to find the travelling Yucatecan always prepared with a personal supply of *chile* in bottled form, brought along for the occasion. Really.

And, finally, while we are on the subject of *chiles,* here's a little conversational clue: *chile* is also a synonym for the male sexual organ, so when you hear a story or one-liner (in Spanish) featuring the word *chile* prominently and everyone laughs, even if you didn't understand the whole thing, you will get the gist. For example, when amongst unknown company that might misinterpret (or laugh at) you, never say:

» *Pásame el chile.*
Pass me the chile.

or even worse:

» *¿Te molesto con el chile?*
Can I bother you with the chile?

china (*CHEE-na*) NOUN—This word is a true local specialty and can mean a couple of things.

1) If you see a sign that says "*100 chinas—17 pesos*" don't go looking for the Chinese girls—*chinas* in this case are oranges. Hence the term *chupar chinas* (to suck oranges). A perfect highway pick-me-up and sold at many a tope throughout the small towns and villages of the Yucatan. As an added bonus you can toss the now-dry half *china* into the jungle at roadside, since it is completely biodegradable.

2) Popular local culture indicates that *china* also refers to the place of origin of anyone who looks Asian. Thus, the tourist from Kyoto, the Hong-Kong-born wife of the multi-millionaire maquiladora owner and the Korean travel agent will all be referred to fondly and generically as *la chinita*.

chino (*CHEE-no*) NOUN, ADJECTIVE—1) The word *chino* does not describe male oranges. Rather, in its NOUN form it is used to refer to anyone of even remotely oriental descent, or that Mexican who has a facial feature generally associated with persons of oriental ancestry, such as the eyes for example. The former and now disgraced president Fujimori of Peru, if he were to visit Merida, would be called *El Chino*. I have a brother-in-law who was called (and sometimes still is) *Chino*, and he calls his son *Chino*, although neither of them are even remotely oriental. Something about the eyes, I guess.

2) In central Mexico, *chino* means curly-haired, so anyone with that characteristic will likely be given the nickname *Chino* while in the Yucatan, anyone with curly hair is a *mulix*. (SEE *mulix*)

chisme (*CHIZ-meh*) GOSSIPY NOUN—*Chisme* is gossip. Hot gossip is *chisme* *caliente*. Everyone loves a good *chisme* or to sit around and *chismear*. If you are known as the go-to source for all gossip, you will be called a *chismosa* possibly to your face and definitely behind your back.

chiva (*CHEE-vah*) ADJECTIVE—Used when you want someone to do something and you have the distinct impression that they really don't want to. In a bank lineup:

> ▶▶ *Ay no seas chiva, págame esto*
> Aw, c'mon please, pay this for me

chivas (*CHEE-vahs*) NOUN—Goats; the Guadalajara soccer team; but for the purposes of this dictionary, it means a bunch of stuff. (SEE ALSO *chucherías*)

> ▶▶ *Voy por mis chivas.*
> I'll get my things.

chivas

chivear (*chih-veh-AHR*) VERB—When you are angry or shy, you are *chiveado* or *chiveada*. The little girl won't come out from behind her Mama's legs to say hello? Probably because she is *chiveada*. Someone is upset because they didn't get what they wanted? They are *chiveado*.

ch'op (*CHOHP*) ADJECTIVE—A Mayan term for the person who has only one working eye, or for the act of poking someone in the eye. Trust me, you won't hear this term anywhere else.

> ▶▶ *Está ch'op.*
> He's only got one eye.

> ▶▶ *¡Uay! ¡Me hicistes ch'op!*
> Hey! You poked me in the eye!

chopim (*CHOH-pim*) VERB—What Yucatecans do when they go to buy clothes and electronics in Houston (SEE *Jiustom*) or Miami to bring back to Merida in fancy suitcases if you're rich and cardboard boxes wrapped in rope if you're not. A good example of the increasing incorporation of English into everyday Spanish, as you can see in the following example:

> ▶▶ *Llévame de chopim a Jiustom.*
> Take me shopping to Houston.

chucherías (*choo-chehr-REE-yahs*) NOUN—Anything, really. A bunch of things piled up in a corner could be a *montón de chucherías*. Or the wife might say to the philandering husband:

> ▶▶ *Agarra tus chucherías y lárgate.*
> Grab your stuff and get the hell out.

chuchú (*choo-CHOO*) NOUN—A female breast, kind of like the English boobs or boobies; a term used by women. Also used when breastfeeding, as in *vamos a darte chuchú* (let's feed you). *Mis chuchús* means "my breasts" as in:

> ▶▶ *¡Me aplastastes mis chuchús!*
> You squished my boobies!

chulísimo (*choo-LEE-see-mo*) ADJECTIVE—Modification of *chulo*, literally "cute." If you are female, you'll want to incorporate this term, which means "fabulous," into your vocabulary when conversing with others, especially those of the *clase acomodada*, who use the word a lot to describe their (and their offspring's) adventures. You have to say it like it meant you had the most fabulous time (even if you are exaggerating just a little). Try to avoid using this word if you are male; you may be suspected of those nasty *costumbres raras*. (SEE *costumbres*)

> ▶▶ *¿Cómo estuvieron tus vacaciones?*
> How were your vacations?

> ▶▶ *¡Ay, amiga, la pasamos chuliiiisimo!*
> Oh they were just faaabulous!

cine (*SEE-neh*) MOVIE NOUN—The local movie theater is *el cine*. Many people go to the *cine* and stand in front of the *cartelera* ("now showing" movie posters) to see what it is they are going to see as they had no plan when they left the house moments ago, dressed up to the nines and emanating strong whiffs of cologne or perfume. For English-speaking foreigners it is good to know that most of the movies, with the exceptions of anything with talking animals or animation (which is obviously for kids who don't speak English), are in English with Spanish subtitles.

clapsurado (*klup-soor-AH-doh*) ADJECTIVE describing something that is closed, as in a pipe or some other form of *tuberia*. A conversation with the *técnico* could go like this:

> ▶▶ *¿Oiga Don Miguel, no puede meter el cable por ahí?*

Hey Miguel, can't you feed the cable through there?

▶▶ *No, Seño, por allá está clapsurada.*
No Ma'am, that way is closed off.

clase acomodada (*CLASS-eh ah-co-mo-DA-da*) The well-off, moneyed folks in Merida. Either through marriage or via a family inheritance, these are the privileged families for whom life is good here. They are featured on the pages of *Diario de Yucatán*'s Plan B supplement, which comes out every Thursday, have one or more *muchachas, mozos,* and *chalánes* at their service, whose kids drive BMWs and Audis and are regulars both in Miami and Houston and at the San Juanistas church. Many are convinced that theirs is the last word in everything from fashion to how to behave in society and often look down upon those less white than themselves, with of course the exception of foreigners and *waches*, who are in a separate and contemptible class of their own; the former often suspected of illicit drug use and dressing inappropriately in public and as for the latter, well they just don't like them. Period.

clínica (*CLEANY-cuh*) NOUN—Any hospital. No one will say they went to *el hospital*, they went to *la clínica*. The Clínica Mérida is traditionally the city's finest hospital; it is the hospital of choice for the elite, the *clase acomodada* and the wannabes. If you go there you will wonder why, since it is a bit of a mess. You will try but be unable to imagine what goes on at the so-called popular hospitals. The newest hospital in Merida as of this writing is the Clínica Star Médica. I had to spend some time there one Christmas and it was a very pleasant stay, according to the people who were there watching me.

Coca (*COH-cah*) NOUN—Shortened version of Coca Cola, like Coke in English speaking countries. *Coca LIE* is the accepted term for a Coca Cola Light, or a Diet Coke. In the case of the latter, you could simply ask for a Diet. For many thousands of Yucatecan babies, *Coca* is the first thing they'll drink after leaving Mom's breast. It is not unusual to see babies sucking on Coca Cola from their baby bottles. They're hooked from that moment onwards and no amount of persuasion by anyone can convince them to drink something else with their meals.

cochera (*coh-CHAIR-ah*) PARKING NOUN—While those fools in Spain say "garaje" (*gah-RAH-heh*) here in the Yucatan, the place to park your car, should you be blessed with such a luxury, especially in the Centro or some of the new micro-housing units scattered around the periphery of Merida, is called a *cochera*. It is the place you put your *coche*.

cola (*COH-lah*) LENGTHY NOUN—The *cola* is literally the tail, usually of an animal that features such an appendage. It is also used here as the word for lineup, as in traffic or at the bank. You might encounter *colas* when waiting to pay for your groceries at the market, waiting for an available bank teller, or in your car at a gas station the night before the hurricane is about to hit and everybody finally believes what the radio and TV have been saying for the last week. The *cola* is also an interesting spring phenomenon at the schools, where mothers (mostly) and fathers (occasionally) will form one outside the school, up to several days before the official inscriptions for the following school year even begin. The local paper, during the month of February, has a photo almost every day of mothers and their plastic chairs in a long *cola*, usually complaining about the wait and the fact that there isn't enough *cupo*. (SEE *cupo*)

If you are in the bank and are not sure if the person in front of you is sort of in the lineup but not really, you can ask him or her "*¿Estás/está en la cola?*" which means "Are you in the lineup?," the former in the familiar *tu* version and the latter in the more polite *usted*.

cochinita (*coh-chee-NEE-tah*) NOUN— Literally "little pig," *cochinita* is the delicious breakfast of choice for Yucatecan partiers everywhere. Served in *tacos* or *tortas*, the greasy pork is marinated in *achiote* (annatto seed paste), which gives it a unique flavour and reddish colour and roasted, traditionally in a pit. From this pit-roasting process comes its full name: *cochinita pibil*. Not to be confused with *lechón*.

cochinita

comida (*coh-MEE-dah*) NOUN—Not just a generic term for food, it is also used to describe the main meal of the day, served between 1 and 3 p.m. On a trip to Chiapas many moons ago, a local Mayan boy acting as a guide referred to food as *el comidas*, charmingly mixing up both the gender and singular/plural of the word.

Comisión, La (*coh-mih-SEEOHN*) NOUN—Term of endearment for the Comision Federal de Electricidad, the federal electricity monopoly that takes care of your electrical power needs in exchange for your first born children. They also keep all those electronic device repair shops in business thanks to their frequent and always inconvenient blackouts, brownouts, and power surges. Their slogan is *"Por el progreso de México,"* which roughly translates "Dedicated to Mexico's progress," which is a pretty optimistic outlook if not an outright falsehood, since the company is really only out to make huge profits for its leaders and government officials and provide free electricity for life for its unionized employees.

That's right, if you work for the CFE, this unique union perk means you can (and they all do) have your AC blasting cold air in your house 24/7 and it won't cost you a thing. At the same time, their public relations machine maintains the print and advertising industry, churning out pamphlets, posters, and banners on how to keep your costs down (buy only food that doesn't require refrigeration, use lights only as a last resort, never blow dry your hair, eat your bread untoasted—that kind of thing).

cómo (*COH-moh*) INTERROGATIVE—The actual word means how, as in:

▶▶ *¿Cómo estás?*
How are you?

But the real purpose of the word's inclusion in this dictionary is the conjugation of *como* with the word *a*. As in *a cómo*. As a new Spanish speaker, or visitor to this fair country or city, you will find things you want to buy and will logically ask how much they cost in the way you would back home: *cuanto cuesta*. Here, however, you show your knowledge of local culture and integration by saying *a cómo*. Some examples:

▶▶ *¿A cómo la papaya?*
How much for the papaya?

▶▶ *¿Cómo salen las papayas?*
How much for the papayas?

And while we are on the subject of price inquiries, another, non-como permutation using qué instead:

▶▶ *¿Qué salen las papayas?*
How much for the papayas?

compac (*COM-puck*) NOUN—This is, you guessed it, a compact disc. While many Mexicans criticize Anglos for being linguistically lazy, there seems to be some evidence that the phenomenon is also present in the formerly "White City" as well as the country at large. Most two-word names will quickly become 50 percent shorter.

▶▶ *¿Ya tienes el nuevo compac de Vritney?*
Have you got Britney's new CD?

confianza (*con-fee-AHN-sah*) NOUN—Trust, confidence. If you have *confianza* with someone, you can divulge more personal information than you would with a recent acquaintance. Uses include:

▶▶ *Le tengo mucha confianza.*
I trust him a lot.

▶▶ *Es de confianza.*
He/she is trustworthy. (Go ahead and tell me what you were going to say.)

▶▶ *personal de confianza*
Staff in a position to receive confidential information within a business environment. Federal labor laws have special clauses for people in these positions.

▶▶ *que falta de confianza*
that lack of trust
(If someone doesn't want to share the latest gossip.)

▶▶ *Abuso de confianza*
Abuse of trust
(As in the person who goes a little too far with confidential information or steals something—money, information, etc.)

confianzudo (*con-fee-AHN-soo-doh*) NOUN—A person who believes that you are his or her confidant and tells you things you don't really want to know about him or herself or others.

▶▶ *Se confía demasiado.*
He trusts a lot.
(Negative connotation here; he/she is going to get screwed.)

conocedor (*coh-noh-seh-DOOR*) CLASSIFYING NOUN—A person who knows. This term is usually found in ads when selling a rare automobile or something of value (watches, jewelry, antiques, books, stereo equipment). The ad commonly contains the phrase *sólo conocedores,* which means that only those who appreciate the value of this weird thing I'm selling should call and others with less taste need not bother. If you were selling your Advent amplifier and Denon CD player, you would insert this phrase, followed by the ridiculously high price that no one from the regular Samsung, Philco, Nagazaki brand market segment would even dream of paying. There is a snobbish implication.

control (*con-TROLL*) NOUN—This is what in Canada and the U.S. is known as the remote, as in remote control:

> ▶ *¿Dónde está el control?*
> Where's the remote?

costumbres (*coss-TOOM-brehs*) NOUN—Customs, traditions, etc. Much was made during the xenophobic days of former governor Victor Cervera's demise on the political landscape, of the *costumbres* of the Yucatecans and how *buenas* they are, as opposed to all that immorality and filth coming from places less virtuous than the land of the pheasant and the deer (all pretty well extinct, by the way). I won't get into all the Yucatecan *costumbres*, since I wrote about those for many years online; it was those *costumbres* that got the website started! I only mention the word because you'll hear it in conversations and in the press as in:

> ▶ *Esa película atenta contra nuestras buenas costumbres.*
> That movie is an affront to our good and noble way of thinking. (They said this about Harry Potter for crying out loud! And heaven forbid that a naked breast should find its way onto your movie screen! But any movie starring Stallone, Van Damme or Schwarzenegger is fine—you figure it out.)

> ▶ *La policía detuvo a una persona de costumbres raras*
> The police apprehended someone strange, e.g. they displayed homosexual tendencies (this is a common one; society in denial!!—as if homosexuality were really that strange in this town.)

creer (*creh-AIR*) VERB—To believe. As in:

> ▶ *Yo creo en Dios.*
> I believe in God.

But an interesting form of the verb is when it is used by Yucatecans to belittle the achievements of other Yucatecans. There is nothing more envy-producing and upsetting to a local than another local who has had some success at something. The whispering and murmuring will begin, as will the attempts at copying the successful individual. The fact that the person now has a better car, a better house, or simply doesn't bitch and moan with the rest of them, results in comments like this one:

>> *Ay sí, se cree.*
Sure, now he thinks he is really something.

Cuba (*COO-bah*)—Tropical Communist rock in the Caribbean—That little island, the festering sore in the track record of the oh-so-successful (!) United States foreign policy, that insists on being pseudo-Communist, is more than all that to the Yucatecans. Mention Cuba at a party and inevitably the subject of those loose Cuban women (and men) comes up and with the lamenting of the local men that their wives won't let them go to Cuba for reasons having to do with marital bliss. There is always someone who someone has heard of or knows who has fallen for one of these extremely attractive women, leaving his wife to bring his new "love" to Merida, only to find that after a few months and having secured her Mexican documents, she has skipped off to Miami to join her relatives already there. Other uses and variations include:

>> *Hay un show cubano nuevo.*
There's a new Cuban show (i.e. let's check out the babes).

>> *Conoció a una cubana.*
He met a Cuban girl (he ran away with a slut).

>> *Estoy tomando clases de salsa con el maestro cubano ese.*
I'm taking salsa lessons with that hot Cuban dance instructor.

cuja (*COO-hah*) NOUN—What the locals call the plastic case your CD is in. According to the *Diccionario Kapelusz*, *cuja* is that little leather pouch on the saddle the flagpole goes into when being carried on horseback, or the one attached to a military uniform in the case of a military honour guard flag bearer. Now, and here in Merida, it holds your Bon Jovi CD. Thanks to my avid reader, Mr. Berny, for this one.

culito (*koo-LEE-toh*) NOUN—A term popularly (and vulgarly I might warn you) used by men to describe an attractive woman. From the vulgar term for that part of her anatomy known in English as her butt—*culo* (SEE *culo*)—it is probably something you don't want to utter in mixed company but can win you the appreciation of your local male friends when used correctly.

> *Mira ese culito.*
> Look at that hot girl.

culo (*COO-loh*) LOWER BACKSIDE BODY PART—While in Spain and other parts of the Spanish-speaking world it would be perfectly acceptable to use the word *culo* in regular conversation, it is considered a swear word in Mexico and Merida is no exception. Literally, it means ass. If someone says something to you that sounds implausible, you might say:

> *Tu culo.*
> Yeah, right.

cupo (*KOO-poh*) NOUN—The term used when you are talking about an available space in relation to the people that want to be in it. At a discotheque or nightclub, you might see a sign indicating *Cupo Limitado*, which means that there is a limit to the number of alcohol-craving human brains that can occupy the space inside the building at any one time. During that time of the year when mothers want to assure a place in the wonderful school system for their offspring, the parental units must, with the help of *primos* (cousins), *vecinos* (neighbours, etc.) form a *cola* (SEE *cola*) to wait for the school inscriptions to begin. Waiting up to a day or two before is not considered unreasonable—imagine wasting this much time in some place like Germany or something. The school will begin "receiving" these mothers until the *cupo* is full. That is the magical moment when the used manila folder appears, that bastion of third-world signage, opened up and pasted on the wall so the rest of the ladies in the line-up can read it, with the message scribbled in thin blue ink in the chicken scratch so favored among Mexican bureaucrats when announcing something last minute: *NO HAY CUPO*. Which means there is no more room, go away.

curioso/a (*koor-ee-OH-soh/sah*) ADJECTIVE—Literally meaning curious or funny, as in kind of strange in a cute way, this adjective can be heard often at hospital maternity wards when the newborn is proudly shown off to relatives and other bystanders. "*¡Ta curioso!*" someone will inevitably exclaim, meaning that they find the baby somewhat aesthetically challenged and while not wanting to hurt the parents' sentiments, feel that unique Yucatecan urge to be honest and not lie about the poor kid's looks.

curiosear (*koor-ee-oh-seh-AHR*) VERB—Stems from the previous word, *curioso*. This verb is applied to those people who go somewhere and walk around, looking curiously at things. For example, in March of 2003, there was a shooting in the Gran Plaza mall—a "crime of passion"—and so the next day many people came to *curiosear*; see what happened. In fact, that's the very term used by the local paper when they reported the incident the following day.

▶ *¿Dónde fuistes?*
Where did you go?

▶ *Fuimos a la Gran Plaza a curiosear.*
We went to the Gran Plaza to have a look around.

D

d (*deh*, also pronounced *theh*)—Fourth letter of the alphabet and also a contender in the grammatical confusion contest. In an effort to show how cosmopolitan they are, many store owners come up with names that in their opinions are so French and worldly sounding. In French, the *D'* (letter *D* followed by an apostrophe) is used when the next word or name begins with a vowel as in *D'Angelo*, or *D'Ivers*. In the land of the pyramid and the *tunkul* (SEE *tunkul*), this practice has been generalized and it is now possible to find such gems as:

➤➤ *D'Williams, D'Marisol, D'Rocio, etc., etc.*

dale (*DAH-leh*)—Commonly used to denote encouragement; promote velocity; hurry things along. If you are watching a basketball game, you might shout "*¡DALE!*" to your favourite player who is chasing the ball. If you are motivating the *albañiles* working for you, you might shout "*¡DALE HIJA!*" to them as they move slowly through their work day. Also, you might mutter "*dale jueputa*" under your breath if they are being particularly obtuse and not moving very quickly. As another example of the usage of this expression, there is the popular children's song to encourage their party guests to break that piñata:

➤➤ *Dale dale dale, no pierdass el tino, porque si lo pierdes, pierdes el camino.*
Basically it means, "Don't aim wrong 'cuz if you do, you'll lose your way."

debedé (*deh-beh-DEH*) NOUN—This is the name of both the electronic device that plays DVDs and the DVD itself. The *debedé* has effectively replaced the *video* (SEE *video*) in most Yucatecans homes.

diario (*dee-AR-ee-yoh*) NOUN—This means newspaper, but for the great majority of Yucatecans, in spite of having several local *diario* options such as *Por Esto, El Financiero, Diario del Sureste,* and the latest incarnation of what was once *Novedades,* the term is used almost exclusively for the *Diario de Yucatán,* Merida's oldest newspaper and the bible for many. To prove a point, a local might say *salió en el Diario,* indicating that there is no doubt as to the veracity of the affirmation made. Interestingly the *Diario*'s penchant of late is to acquire news directly off peoples' or organizations Facebook pages. For local gossip buffs, the *Diario* was founded by the Menendez family and one of the family members broke rank and founded the *Por Esto* newspaper, which spends an inordinate amount of ink and paper on criticizing the owners and content of the *Diario.* For politics fans, note that the *Diario* is known as being *PANista* while the *Por Esto* favors the PRI party.

Disney (DEESS-*nay*) NAME—This is the park where the mouse lives and *visita obligada* for all well-off Yucatecans many of whom are unable or unwilling to stretch their imaginations any further and visit the park over and over, ad nauseum.

don (*don*) NOUN—SALUTATION. Used much like "mister" in English, along with *señor.* While *señor* is used with the last name as in *Señor* Calderon, *don* is used with the first name: *Don* Felipe. Among folks from rural areas with limited education, there is some confusion and you will hear *Don* Calderon. In a service situation, the person behind the counter may ask:

> ▸ *¿Qué le damos, don?*
> What can I get you, sir?

doña (DON-*yah*)—The female version of *don.* Don't be surprised when you magically transform from the boring and so-not-you Mrs. Peterson, to the more personal and intimate *Doña* Kathy.

Dzibilchaltun (*dzee-beel-chahl-TOON*) MAYAN SITE—I do not intend to list every Mayan site in the state of Yucatan, but thought I would include a few of the main ones due to their proximity to the city of Merida and this one in particular as people seem to have a hard time pronouncing it (SEE ALSO *Oxcutzcab*), thereby providing a valuable public service. Tip for the would-be visitor: avoid Mondays and Wednesdays, as these are the days when cruise ships dock in Progreso and hordes of tourists descend *en masse* at the site and make a peaceful swim in the *cenote* impossible what with all their screaming and splashing.

dzonot (*dzoh-NOHT*) REFRESHING NOUN—Mayan word from which the Spanish, in their inept attempts to turn the Mayan language into their native Castilian, created the commonly known "cenote" (SEE *cenote*). Like the word "tun" (SEE *tun*) *dzonot* is often found in names of villages and towns on the highways and byways of the Yucatan indicating that there is a *cenote* in the vicinity. On a hot day, this is welcome news indeed so stop and explore.

E

e (*eh*)—Fifth letter of the alphabet and the sound it makes is an expression of incredulity, if incredulity is a word. For example, person A is telling person B that a third person has just won the lottery, sold their house or car at an extremely good price. Upon hearing this, person B exclaims "¡EH!" However, if the information is unbelievable and the listener feels some doubt as to its veracity, the *eh* will be followed by a laconic *"ta bueno."* For example:

> *Mi hermano fue el presidente de España.*
> My brother was the president of Spain.

> *Eh, ta bueno.*
> Sure he was.

edificio (*eh-dih-FEESS-eeyoh*) NOUN—If you have ever chatted with the traffic cop on the corner about something other than getting out of a traffic violation, he will perhaps mention the *edificio*. This is the term used for their headquarters—the equivalent of "downtown" to an urban cop in the U.S. If he commits some kind of impropriety, he is taken to the *edificio*. (While we're on the subject of law enforcement, SEE ALSO *elemento*.)

Ek Balam (*EK-bah-LAHM*) MAYAN SITE—Close to Valladolid, this Mayan site features some interesting stuccos on its large pyramid, which as of this writing, you can still climb. There is a *cenote* nearby but the best part of the trip is a stop in nearby Temozon for smoked meat and *longaniza* (SEE *longaniza*) *tacos*.

eléctrico (*eh-LEK-trick-oh*) SHOCKING NOUN—There seems to be some confusion about the term among some locals, particularly men when discussing masculine themes related to home or car repair. You may hear this word used (incorrectly) in reference to an electrician, the translation for which is actually *electricista*.

elemento (*eh-leh-MEN-toh*) NOUN—In the officious government language used by the police, this is what they call themselves.

▸ *Yo y otro elemento fuimos al lugar de los hechos.*
Myself and a fellow officer went to the scene of the crime.

empacar (*em-pah-CAHR*) VERB—To pack. As in suitcases and boxes tied with string for international travellers. Also used to describe the act of voluminous eating; if you see someone getting up from a table and holding his stomach and looking pained, you might comment:

▸ *¿Te empacaste unas cuantas tortas verdad?*
You wolfed down a couple of *tortas,* didn't you?

emposmado (*em-pohs-MAH-doh*)—The inflated state of your stomach. Imagine having eaten several helpings of *frijol con puerco*, accompanied by a beer or three and then having a Coke for dessert. How would your stomach look? Pretty distended right? Lots of gas, right? Well this is what being *emposmado* is all about. And those folks, who have a permanent bulge around their middle, insist that they are not fat, they are simply *emposmado,* implying a transient nature to their expanded waistline.

encabronado (*en-cab-roh-NAH-do*) ANGRY ADJECTIVE—When you are very angry, really pissed off, you are *encabronado*. A variation of this is *encabritado*, which is a little lighter because it doesn't involve the use of the goat-reference *cabrón*, which is generally accepted as being a "bad" word. Again, not to be used in polite company.

▸ *Estoy encabronado/a.*
I'm so pissed off.

enchilar (*enn-chih-LAHR*) VERB—This is what happens when you overdo it with the *chile.* Your mouth is on fire, your eyes are watering, your nose is dripping and beads of sweat are forming on your forehead. At this point you would exclaim:

▸ *¡UAY! ¡Me enchilé!*
Holy flaming lips, Batman! I'm dying here!

enchilar

enfermar (*enn-fehr-MAHR*) VERB—To get sick. Nevertheless, in the pueblos of Yucatan, you will hear pregnant women refer to their upcoming delivery as the day they are going to *enfermar* or get sick. The most interesting use of the verb I have heard so far, was in a conversation I had with a fellow cleaning my office, who remarked that his son had made pregnant his girlfriend. What he said was:

▶▶ *Mi hijo enfermó a su novia.*
My son got his girlfriend pregnant.

The other use is:

▶▶ *Voy a enfermar.*
I'm pregnant and/or I will be delivering a baby soon.

Escosham (*eh-SCOH-shum*) NOUN—There is something mysterious here about words that begin with the letter *S* which turns an innocuously named Canadian bank originally from Nova Scotia into this aberration.

▶▶ *¿A dónde vas?*
Where are you going?

▶▶ *Voy al Escosham.*
I'm off to Scotiabank.

Eskai (*ess-KYE*) NOUN—Commercial name of DirecTV's competition for your satellite TV peso. *Eskai* features the programming of Televisa, the culturally demented mega-consortium broadcasting *wach* culture (SEE *wach*) to all of Mexico, parts of the U.S. and Latin America. Its quality is only one rung above the Venezuelan programming, which has to be the worst in the world. As of this writing, DirecTV is no longer available in Mexico. The latest satellite offering is Dish Network, for Mexico, which means that it's not the American crap you will get to see, but the Mexican crap.

especial (*ess-pess-ee-YAHL*) ADJECTIVE—A person whose personality is very conflictive and problematic, or extremely eccentric to the point of being a sociopath, would be called *especial*. Definitely special indeed.

espectacular (ess-peck-tah-coo-LAHR)—You'd think it was an adjective but it's a NOUN—the myriad gigantic billboards you see EVERYwhere around Merida, particularly on the Progreso highway, are called *espectaculares*. Why? Maybe because they're so spectacularly distracting and make for some spectacular visual contamination.

Estarbuk (*eh-STAR-book*) NOUN—Since the arrival of Starbucks coffee in Merida I have heard its name mangled on many occasions. This is the most popular mangling.

THE MODERN YUCATAN DICTIONARY

etiqueta *(eh-tee-KEH-tah)* ADJECTIVE—The word means label or sticker, but it is used when penning invitations and the maximum formality is desired e.g. tuxedo *(SEE ALSO smoking)* for the men and evening gown for the ladies. Usually accompanied by the term *rigurosa*, which means rigorous, or, in other words, don't dare to show up in just a suit and tie or worse, a blazer and no tie. Although invitations occasionally indicate *rigurosa etiqueta*, you may be surprised at the amount of people who disregard such indications and show up in a suit and tie. This is Merida after all, where no one really minds and besides, the climate is not entirely compatible with the formal attire so common elsewhere.

F

faltar (*fahl-TAHR*) VERB—What the person you hired to do work around the house or, if you are a business person, the person(s) you hired to be your employees will eventually do. *Faltar al trabajar* means not showing up at work, and this happens a lot. Keep track of the excuses given, as you may find that a worker who doesn't show up on a regular basis may seem to have a lot of sick *abuelas* (grandmothers). It is imperative to immediately set the tone of how missing work will be handled—if you are weak and "nice" you are going to have a lot of problems in the future.

fomentar (*foh-men-TAHR*) VERB—Among the people who live in the rural areas of Yucatan, when you are cleaning a piece of land, perhaps preparing it for the planting of corn or other crops, you are *fomentando* it. When driving by a lot recently, where a backhoe was clearing away those nasty garbage producing trees and other nuisances, the campesino woman accompanying us commented:

▶▶ *¿Este terreno lo están fomentando, verdad?*
They are clearing/cleaning/preparing this piece of land, right?

foreigner (*fohr-REYG-nehr*)—Read the pronunciation again. This is how the name of a popular 80's band is pronounced in Spanish.

francés (*frun-CESS*) NOUN—This classic Yucatecan bakery staple, resembles (surprise) a French loaf of bread! In many a pueblo and among Meridas' so-called "popular" social classes, you will hear the phrase *Ve a comprar francés*, which does not mean that a Frenchman is in town and is up for sale. It simply means, run along to the bakery and pick up some bread. Best when topped with plenty of greasy *cochinita*, i.e. roast pork.

fregado (*freh-GAH-doe*) ADJECTIVE—(SEE ALSO *fregar*) *Fregado* is someone or something that has been beat up (by life, overuse, the normal course of time, excessive interest on that bank loan, etc.) *Fregado* can be subsituted with *jodido*, which is a little stronger and certainly not for use in mixed company or introductory conversations.

▶ *¿Viste a Juan?*
Did you see Juan?

▶ *Sí hombre; está bien fregado.*
Sure did; man, does he ever look like shit.

fregar (*freh-GAHR*) VERB (SEE below for the original meaning)—To screw someone. Not in the sexual sense, but in the sense of obtaining advantage over an imagined (or real) adversary. Say you on are on Montejo roundabout, stuck at a light. If you are in the right lane, you can pretend to turn right, as you may do so on a red light, and then suddenly turn left and back onto Montejo to continue on, thereby avoiding waiting like all those suckers you have just *fregar-d*. Other examples of usage include:

▶ *Me lo fregué.*
I sure got him.

▶ *Me está fregando.*
He's bugging me.

▶ *Es un fregón.*
He's a pest.

▶ *Me dió un fregadazo.*
He belted me (either physically or by taking advantage of me in a major way).

fregastes, te (*freh-GAHS-tess*) VERB—You're screwed! From the Spanish *fregar*, which actually means to clean up (in Spain they still use it as such), proof of which is the *fregadero* or sink. If you are a student and you didn't hand in your assignment on time, although you beg and plead, the teacher won't accept it and tells you *¡Pues te fregastes!* meaning you're outta luck. The *s* on the end is a Yucatecan or perhaps Mexican invention among the linguistically challenged; the correct term would be *fregaste*.

fresco 1) (*FRESS-coe*) NOUN—*El fresco* is what you "take" when you drag your wooden or plastic white chairs onto the sidewalk in front of your downtown home, say in the Santiago area, and sit there, chatting with family and friends or neighbours, watching the cars and pedestrians go by. It's called *fresco* because the temperature does drop a little after the sun goes down and this popular quaint activity can still be observed in some parts of downtown and the south of Merida. In the well-off northern neighbourhoods like Colonia Mexico, Monte Cristo, and the like, the advent of air conditioning and more recently, the casinos, has made the practice all but obsolete. *Fresco* is also when the temperature has dropped to the point where the heat is no longer crushing you, and you step outside after a late-night party for example and exclaim *"maare, hay fresco,"* indicating that you feel a slight chill.

2) ADJECTIVE—The term is used to describe that person that takes advantage of you or someone else. As in:

▶▶ *Dejó su auto a propósito para que yo la lleve.*
She left her car on purpose so that she could hitch a ride with me.

▶▶ *¡Ay qué fresco!*
Translation unknown!

A variation of the word is *frescura*, which literally means "freshness," but in this context denotes the act of being *fresco*.

Fresco can also be used to describe something that is cool to the touch, like a can of soda pop or beer.

▶▶ *¿Esta helada?*
Is it ice cold?

▶▶ *No, pero está fresca.*
No, but it's cool.

fulano (*foo-LAHN-oh*) GENERIC NOUN—*Fulano* is the name of the person (male is *fulano*, female is *fulana*) whose name you don't know, have forgotten, or are talking about and could care less what his name is at all. When there are two of these persons, the second one is always called *mengano* (SEE *mengano*). You might be describing an incident at a nightspot, for example.

▶▶ *Luego vino ese fulano . . .*
So then that guy comes along . . .

G

gabacho (*gah-BAH-cho*) NOUN—(SEE ALSO *gringo*; same thing.) Almost never heard in Merida, you will hear it all the time in nearby Cancun. The female version is *gabacha*.

gastar (*guss-TAHR*) VERB—1) To finish something. In Merida, when you finish a beer, you say:

> *Se gastó mi cerveza.*

And when you have polished off all the Coronas, you can say:

> *Se gastó toda la cerveza.*

If you find that you have no more pesos for beer and want someone to buy you another, you can say:

> *Es que se me gastó el dinero.*

When you're out of time and you know your wife will be waiting with your suitcases packed to kick you out of the house for being away drinking so long, you can say:

> *Se me gastó el tiempo.*

If your friends wonder why you're leaving without finishing your beer, they might ask:

> *¿No la vas a gastar?*

This is as opposed to se *acabó la cerveza/el dinero/el tiempo*, which is probably the more correct term. Other uses include:

> *Es que la pieza estaba muy gastada.*
> The part (think auto mechanics) was worn out.

> *¡Se te va a gastar!*
> It's going to run out! (a kid drinking his soda pop too quickly).

> *¡Gástalo!*
> Finish it! (You are leaving the restaurant and someone hasn't finished their meal or drink and you already paid for it!)

2) To spend money. If you are shopping, you are *gastando dinero*. The meager household allowance, given to the wife by the husband who has spent most of his paycheck in the cantina, is called *el gasto*. This is probably not so much a Yucatecan thing, but you will hear it.

3) Expense. Your satellite TV subscription is a *gasto*, as is your monthly telephone bill and the bi-monthly CFE assault on your pocketbook.

glorieta (*glory-YET-ah*) ROUNDABOUT NOUN—Most Latin American cities have some, a remnant from the Spanish who made their avenues wide and then plopped monuments of famous people in the middle of them. To get around these, traffic circles were invented or evolved. In Merida, and most likely other places as well, they are called *glorietas* and in 2011 the municipal authorities thought it would be swell to get rid of one on the Prolongacion del Paseo de Montejo (called the Burger King *glorieta* because of its proximity to the Home of the Whopper) and build an underpass instead, because they wanted to "modernize" the city and make traffic more "fluid." Never mind that there are about 997,542 other things the enormous amount of money used could have modernized and that the underpass will not solve any traffic problem, thanks to non-synchronized traffic lights on every end of each of the lanes going into, and out of, the underpass.

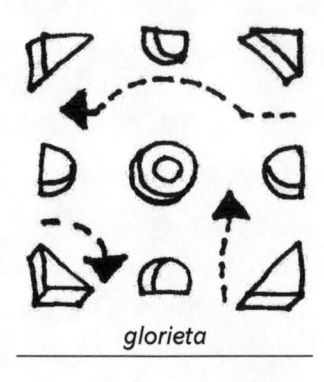

glorieta

gorda (*GOHR-duh*) ADJECTIVE—A term of endearment among Mexican men. To call your wife "fatty" can be dangerous in some marital situations, but in many Mexican relationships it is perfectly acceptable. *Gordo*, the male version of the same thing, is more common and seems to me anyway, a little less offensive. Some women will even call other women's men *gordo*, once a bit of *confianza* has been established. This is however, to me anyway, crossing a line. Don't use it when starting out in society.

gratis (*GRAH-teess*) ADJECTIVE—One of the favorite words of many Yucatecans who love to find a bargain (to the point of sacrificing everything else) and for those who are notoriously cheap. If something is announced as *gratis*, then there will be a rush to get it, whatever it may be and regardless of whether or not it is actually needed. Usually used in an incredulous tone of voice as in:

> *¡Son gratis, amiga!*
> They're free!

grey (*GREY*) NOUN—There is a type of grapefruit grown in the Yucatan, very large and fibrous but in general a grapefruit nevertheless, and you might here it called a *grey*. Obviously this comes from the English.

gringo (*GREEN-go*) NOUN—Anyone obviously non-Mexican gets thrown into this category, although some neurotic Canadians try to make the distinction that they are not *gringos*, that the term applies only to those from the United States. There is a negative implication to being a gringo in many cases, although it can be used as a term of relative endearment. *La gringuita* is that American woman who bought the *hacienda* and is generally nice to everyone, although we know she's kind of naïve and crazy. We like her and everything and every year she buys Christmas presents for the local village children, but we still "borrow" stuff from the *hacienda* when she is not there and then forget to return it. But she is nice.

guácala (*WAH-cah-lah*) EXPRESSION—If something is gross, vomit inducing and totally gnarly, like going to visit some long lost relative in some exciting locale like Campeche, your local teenager might blurt out *¡guácala!*, indicating his or her displeasure with the mere notion of being included in such a mundane family activity.

güey (*WAY*) NOUN—More and more these days, the customs of the Yucatecans are being overrun by those nasty *waches* and this expression comes straight from the land of the hated D.F. itself. A term for "bro" or "man," it is simply added to the end of any salutation or affirmation indiscriminately. Lately, even girls have taken to calling each other *güey*, which just sounds strange, at least to me. Especially when Every. Second. Word. Is. *Guey*. Not a term to be used when trying to endear oneself to a die-hard *Yuca*. Avoid this one.

guindar (*ginn-DAHR*) VERB—Literally, to hang. You are infinitely more likely to learn the verb *colgar* in your Spanish class, but in the Yucatan (and Tabasco, Campeche, and other states in the area) you can and will hear the word *guindar* used, usually in reference to the hanging of a hammock. I have also heard it used in reference to the business practice of spending all your income without thinking about covering your costs and resupplying:

» *Se está guindando de su negocio.*
He is sucking the cash flow out of his business.

And also this question, which I heard after someone had hung up some shirts:

» *¿Están bien guindadas?*
Are they hung up right?

gustar (*goose-TAHR*) VERB—To like. I have personally witnessed innumerable occasions where Merida's well off, also know as the *clase acomodada,* and *waches* (SEE *wach*) now residing in Merida, have made fun of this verb, used almost exclusively by their *muchachas* and *mozos* and other members of their indispensable *servicio* staff. You see, the people from the pueblos don't watch or look at (*mirar*) or even see (*ver*) the TV, they *gustar* it; as in:

» *¿Juanito, que estabas haciendo?*
What were you doing, Juanito?

» *Nada, estaba gustando la novela.*
Nothing, I was watching the soap opera.

H

hacendado (*ah-sen-DAH-doh*) IMPORTANT NOUN—The *hacendado* was the owner of the *hacienda* (SEE *below*). Back in the good old days when the Spanish "discovered" the area, the Spanish Crown awarded the thugs, former prisoners, and drunken sailors with large tracts of land called *encomiendas* that they then used to build themselves *haciendas*. It is said that just 50 families owned most of the land (and those pesky little brown people who came with it) in the Yucatan before there was land reform and the Mayans became revolting.

hacienda (*ah-see-YEN-dah*) NOUN—A large tract of land with an imposing set of structures built thereon usually including—but not limited—to a main house of varying degrees of opulence for the European owners, a machine room, storage areas, and Mayan workers houses. Originally cattle ranches and farming operations, the *haciendas*, or plantations, were converted to *henequén* (SEE *henequén*) production when an efficient method of extracting fibre from the plant became available and the Yucatan supplied rope and other *sisal* products to the world.

As a result of land reform laws started in 1915, which returned the land occupied by the Europeans and their descendants to the original owners, the Indians, followed by the of plastic on the ropemaking scene, the *hacienda* operation became economically unviable and many were abandoned.

Today, *haciendas* are luxury hotels, restaurants, and locations rented out for social events, and are the model for both official and private sector announcements that extoll the virtues of Yucatans glorious past, thereby completely overlooking the violent oppression of the vast majority of the peninsula's inhabitants, the Mayans.

heladés (*ell-ah-DESS*) NOUN—When the months of October through February come around, the weather, besides being wet and subject to the occasional hurricane, gets a little chilly for the locals. While the Canadian tourists from Toronto and other frigid places in the Great

White North frolic in the waves in Progreso, the locals are wrapped in moldy sweaters with their arms folded protectively in front of them. "*Hay heladés*" is a comment heard often during these months, especially in the mornings. Air conditioning is also a cause of *heladé*s; some particularly thin-blooded locals go so far as to wear a sweater when shopping at Sam's Club, or when going to the movies, where they try to sit somewhere where they are not going to get hit by the air coming from the vents.

henequén (*en-eh-KEN*) NOUN—The fibre extracted from the agave plant of the same name native to the Yucatan (SEE ALSO *sisal*). The Mayans used to retrieve the fibre manually but during the time of the haciendas, the wealthy hacienda owners converted their cattle ranches and fruit orchards to the cultivation of the henequén plant and invented machines to extract the fibre, in response to the world demand for rope, especially for the shipping industry. This economic activity, which resulted in more millionaires here than anywhere else in the world at the time, put Yucatan on the map and is why there is still evidence of extreme wealth in the city of Merida and in the haciendas dotting the countryside. It all came to a crashing halt when plastic was invented and land reform laws were passed almost at the same time. The fact that the Mayans were no longer allowed to be used as slaves also had something to do with the decline of the lifestyles of the rich and famous. Many of Yucatan's most powerful families can trace their lineage back to fortunes built on the backs of Mayan workers.

hermoso/a (*air-MOH-so/sah*) ADJECTIVE—Someone who is fat is *hermoso*! So the literal meaning, beautiful, is not exactly what the person paying the "compliment" has in mind. Babies are *hermosos* and considered healthy when fed corn syrup to fatten them up. This interpretation of the word, popular in the pueblos, probably comes from years of poverty when babies were scrawny little bony things and the image of the fat babies of the rich was considered the ideal, both aesthetically and for health reasons. *Una muchacha hermosa* means a chubby, rosy cheeked, young girl.

huach (SEE *wach*)

hueva (*WEH-bah*) NOUN—1) Fish roe, usually served in seafood buffets or at beachside palapa restaurants in Progreso. La Pigua, that bastion of seafood culinary excess, makes a delicious *salsa de hueva* that they use on shrimp and fish fillets.

2) The sleepy feeling you get after a superb meal in which you've stretched your stomach way beyond its normal capacity, and are in dire need of repose. Usually *la hueva* hits you in the afternoon after the midday meal. It is increasingly used as an excuse during any time of the day however, to get out of doing something. Keep in mind that the term is not entirely socially acceptable and should not be used on a first date, or when substitute teaching at Harmon Hall English school. Some possible uses of the word are:

▸▸ *Me da hueva.*
I'm too lazy.

▸▸ *Me está dando una hueva.*
I feel a nap coming on.

Variations of the term exist, and should be recognized as stemming from the original. These include, but are not limited to:

▸▸ *La hora de la uva.*
A politer way of saying that it's nap time; note the insertion of the *uva* instead of *hueva*.

▸▸ *huevón*
This is the guy who is permanently napping and lazy as hell.

▸▸ *ueyvis (WAVE-ees)*
Another derivation of hueva.

huevo (*WEH-voe*) NOUN—This is of course, the egg. In modern and not very polite Spanish, eggs are also testicles, resulting in all kinds of permutations, most of which you can imagine for yourself. Here are, however, some examples:

huevo

▸▸ *¿Qué haces?*
What are you doing?

▸▸ *Rascando los huevos.*
Scratching my scrotum (i.e. doing nothing).

▸▸ *Le faltaron huevos para decir lo que tenía que decir.*
He didn't have the nerve to say what he should have said.

Along these lines is the expression *a huech/a wech*, which is the SLANG term for a *huevo*.

huiro *(WEE-roe)* SIMPLE NOUN—In some parts of the Spanish speaking world, a *huiro* or *guiro* is an instrument. In the Yucatan a *huiro* (*huira* for the women) is someone with no class, an ignorant person. Used much the same as indio *(SEE indio)*.

▶▶ *Compré unos lentes Prada.*
I bought some Prada glasses.

▶▶ *¿Qué es Prada?*
What's Prada?

▶▶ *¿¡No sabes qué es Prada?! ¡¡Eres más huira!!*
You don't know what Prada is?! You're so ignorant!!

I

iich (*ITCH*) NOUN—A very good, close friend. This is a Mayan term used often in the Yucatan; there was at one point even a glossy magazine full of pictures of "nice" (read society) people having fun, called *Iiches*.

> ▶ *Esa Juanita es mi iich.*
> That Juanita is my very dear friend.

impermeable (*im-pehr-meh-AH-bleh*) NOUN—This means what it means in English also; in Merida, however, it refers to the thing you wear if there is the threat of rain on the horizon, or it is already wet outside, and you don't want to get soaked. If it is raining and you are wet, someone will invariably ask you:

> ▶ *¡Uay! ¿No trajistes tu impermeable?*
> OMG! You didn't bring a raincoat?

india (*IN-deeya*) NOUN, ADJECTIVE—Even in this 21st century, in the class conscious, limited world view of certain Yucatecans, anyone with a Mayan surname and or excessively brown complexion is called un *indio* or una *india* (SEE ALSO *naca, naco*). This is not a Yucatecan phenomenon of course; it's prevalent throughout the country. Also, if someone does something that is so lacking in perceived class or "good" taste, they are accused of being an *indio*. For example:

> ▶ *¿¡Cómo pudiste hacer eso?! Eres una india.*
> How could you do that?! You are such a loser.

inge (*IN-heh*) NOUN—In Mexico everyone has a title. No one is simply *Señor* Perez. He is the C.P. (*contador público* or public accountant) doctor or whatever. *Inge* is a short term of endearment for the ever-popular *ingeniero*, or engineer (which can be applied to other professions as well such as *Lic* (*LICK*) for *Licenciado*, *Arqui* (*AR-kee*) for architect, etc.). In Mexico, *ingeniero* is an extremely popular career choice for many males, and when you have a cordial relationship with one, you can greet him as follows:

» *¿Qué pasó, inge?*
What's up, engineer?

A fellow I know, an architect, always greets me using the above salutation. Apparently, he has to call me SOMEthing, although I have never displayed any engineering tendencies, to my knowledge.

J

j (*HOE-tah*)—The letter which is pronounced like a *y* in Merida. Thereby, Jessica becomes Yessica, Janet (or Janeth) becomes Yanet, etc. which makes for some interesting names when you are reading the social pages of the local paper.

jala (*HAH-lah*) VERB—This verb, when used in its imperative form, is used to aggressively encourage people to move along. If you are trying to get some folks out of your living room where they have staged a protest, or some stray dogs from your porch, or the neighbours' kids out of your mango tree, you yell at them "*Jala jala!*" while moving both arms in violent swinging motions indicating the general direction in which they are to move. If you watch subtitled television, *jala* appears as *hala*. Why this is I do not know. It looks weird though.

Since *jala* is the first pair of syllables in the name of a Yucatecan town called Halacho, this is used by some in the same context:

▸▸ *¡Empacamos y Halacho!*
Let's pack up and move out!

Jiustom (*HEW-stom*) NOUN—A very important city in the state of Texas, where many Yucatecans live, and many more travel to do some *chopim* (SEE ALSO: *chopim*).

joder (*hoe-DEHR*) FILTHY CUSS VERB—The English equivalent would be "fuck," with all the versatility of that word and then some. Its original meaning is usually defined as to copulate, but there are so many more wonderful ways to use the word. Some examples include:

▸▸ *Me lo jodí.*
I sure got him.

▸▸ *Es un jodón.*
He's a pest.

> *¡No (me) jodes!*
> Don't fuck (me) around.

> *Estoy jodido.*
> I'm screwed.

and so many more!

joto (*HOH-toh*)—Yet another word for a male of the gay persuasion. Amazing how many of these there are in this macho society, isn't it?

jueputa (SEE *ueputa*)

K

k (*KAH*) The letter *k* is virtually non-existant in the language of Cervantes, but you will hear words beginning with *k* in the Yucatan—Mayan words! Here is a taste of some of the more popular and oft-heard ones.

kau (*COW*) BLACK, NOISY NOUN—The ubiquitous grackle that descends upon the large green trees in Merida's plazas and main avenues is called a *kau*, or *x'kau*, the "x" prefix being the accepted way to contemptualize (author's own term) any word (SEE X). The male *kau* is the noisiest—the sounds vary from elongated shrieks to guttural squawks and short machine-gun bursts of throaty clacks—and is jet black and very unafraid of humans, while the female is a little more reserved, smaller, and a faded brown color. In the Holiday Inn parking lot, an area under the leafy trees that becomes home to the birds at night displays a warning sign that reads *Zona de Aves*. In other words, you may need a serious car washing the next day if you park your car here.

kau

kis (*KEESS*) SMELLY NOUN—It is a source of endless amusement when Mayan speaking Spanish students learning English discover that the English "kiss" is the word for a romantic meeting of lips because, in the Mayan language a very similar-sounding word *kis* means, to put it bluntly, fart.

kisin (*kih-SEEN*) EVIL NOUN—The *kisin* is the devil. It is not unusual to hear parents utter ¡*mejen kisin!* with regards to their own or another's offspring. This simply means that the child in question is a terror.

kisin

THE MODERN YUCATAN DICTIONARY

ko'ox (*coh-OSH*) VERB—Let's go. This is one Mayan expression that is very popular to this day, even used among the well-off in every age bracket who often include the English "let's" as in "let's go" to form the hybrid *let's ko'ox* when expressing their desire to get up and move along. The correct Mayan usage is for one other person besides yourself. If there is more than one person to be invited to go, the term would be *ko'onex*.

k'ol (*KOHL*) NOUN—A white pasty gravy made with corn starch and chicken or turkey stock and served with the authors favourite Yucatecan dish, *queso relleno*, or stuffed cheese. *K'ol* can be found in other dishes as well and you will see it on menus in restaurants featuring food from the region.

L

lado (*LAH-doh*) NOUN—Side. *Un lado* means one side, while *el otro lado* means the other side, often used to describe the other side of the border, i.e. the U.S.A. There are some other uses for the word. Here are two:

▶▶ If you have a store or business and have enjoyed a great day where you have sold a lot, you supposedly have a lot of money in your pocket and *te vas de lado*, which means that you are loaded with cash and the weight is making you walk with one side lower than the other.

▶▶ Another use for *lado* is the "other side" usage. If someone is *del otro lado* i.e. the other side, it means he is a homosexual. Notice how the homosexual concept keeps coming up in this supposedly macho society? Interesting.

lana (*LAH-nah*)—The SLANG term, originating probably in the central region of Mexico, for money. Used by urban *Yucas* and those in contact with people from other parts of the country; not heard so often in villages where the Mayan language predominates and where outside influence is minimal.

▶▶ *No traigo lana.*
I have no cash.

lastimada (*lahs-tee-MAH-dah*) NOUN—From the verb *lastimar*, to hurt or cause pain. The correct Spanish term would be *herida* (wound) but if you have a scratch on your forehead you have a *lastimada* (a hurt). Used mostly by mothers when speaking to their offspring. Also known in some circles as *yaya*. Adults don't have *lastimadas*, especially adult males. They have *putazos, chingadazos, madrazos*, etc.

Las Begonias (*Lahs-Beh-GOHN-yahs*) PLACE NAME—This is what locals colloquially call that desert city filled with gambling and vice in Nevada. Many rich Mexican politicians visit Las Begonias in September, travelling on taxpayer-funded expense accounts and gambling away exceedingly large amounts of taxpayer money that should have gone to roads, hospitals, schools; that sort of thing. I have seen this first hand, up close and personal. You will too, if you visit Vegas in September.

lechón (*leh-CHONE*) NOUN—Roast suckling pig. Absolutely delicious on toasty *francés* bread.

levantar (*leh-vun-TAHR*) VERB—To raise, lift up, etc. In Yucatan, this verb also means to put something away for safekeeping; money, valuables, an important list. Probably comes from the Mayan village culture, where the floor is dirt and furniture is rare. Usually there might be a little shelf or simply a place to hang something from a branch that forms part of the palapa roof. Example:

>> *¿Ya metistes tu dinero al banco?*
Did you put your money in the bank?

>> *No, lo tengo levantado.*
No, I have put it away.

Levantar also has a meaning related to clearing up. After a meal, the *muchacha* (you didn't think a family member would do it, did you?) will be asked to *levantar la mesa*. Translated literally, the poor girl would be forced to lift the table either through brute strength or some Copperfieldian illusion; but in the Yucatan, she is being asked to clear everything off the table.

libre (*LEE-breh*) ADJECTIVE—Literally, free. As in a seat on the bus, admission to a cultural event sponsored by the government, etc. etc. In Yucatan, it is also used by the *mene mene* men (SEE *mene mene*) to indicate to you, along with vigorous red rag swinging, that the coast is clear. Also, there are two highways from Merida to Cancun, one is the *libre*, which means you don't have to pay any tolls.

ligar (*lee-GAHR*)—JOINING VERB—Literally, to tie up. If your fallopian tubes have been tied, you are *ligada*. The other, more common use of this word is in reference to meeting and hooking up with someone of the opposite sex. It is common to hear young males bragging when they went to Cancun:

>> *Me ligué una gringa.*
I hooked up with a gringa.

loch (*LOCH*) NOUN/VERB—Pronounced hard and fast, it is in fact a Mayan word for something soft and slow—a tender hug. *Hacer loch* is to be in the state of hugging someone. It is a word that has become fully integrated in the Yucatecan spoken Spanish, although some misguided folks think that *loch* is a little more daring and sexually oriented.

> ¿Me haces loch?
> Can you give me a hug?

Interestingly, people from central Mexico cannot say *loch*. They have a problem with the *ch* sound and pronounce it *losh*.

lograda (*loh-GRAH-dah*) ADJECTIVE—Achieved; a unique use for this word came up when a lady in a pueblo was asking about my daughters and how old they were. When I answered that they were in their early teens, the woman exclaimed with a dismissive wave and triumphant tone of voice, *"Ah, ya están logradas,"* probably meaning that the fun associated with ear infections and diapers was over and done with. Nothing to worry about, they're *logradas*!

longaniza (*lohn-gah-NEE-sah*) SMOKED NOUN—Most people from reasonably cosmopolitan places across the globe have heard of *chorizo*; *longaniza* is its shy close cousin. Heavily condimented but rarely spicy ground pork sausage, cooked slowly over heat and smoke until wrinkled and dried-out looking. Best served up fried in a pan until the skin is crispy, along with some refried beans, handmade tortillas, cooked tomato salsa and roasted pickled onions. The best place to sample and buy this sausage to take home is the tiny hamlet of Temozon, on the road between Valladolid and Tizimin, which is also the road to the Mayan site of Ek Balam (SEE *Ek Balam*)

Los Miamis (*lohs-my-AH-mees*) PLACE NAME—Another city, this one in Florida, where locals love to shop and stay at hotels like the dark and spooky Everglades and the cockroach-infested DeLido because they're cheap. This term is used mostly by those locals that travel there; the so-called *clase acomodada* or their wannabe hangers-on.

M

ma (*mah*) "No," in Mayan. The popular phrase that defines the stubbornness of the Yucatecans is

>> *¡Cuando digo ma es ma!*
> When I say no, I mean no!

maare (*MAH-ray*) YET ANOTHER CLASSIC YUCA EXPRESSION— Used when you are either impressed or perhaps frustrated. Someone showing off their shiny new car (complete with the plastic seat covers still in place to protect the cloth)? *Maaare*. New and very attractive girlfriend? *Maaare*. Trip to the *extranjero* and you know you can't afford to go? *Maaare*. Usually said while jutting out the lower lip and nodding one's head slowly.

>> *¡Maare, está enorme!*
> Holy smokes; it's huge!

Also used as a term of affirmation in a resigned sort of way as in

>> *¿Te pegó duro lo del banco verdad?*
> That bank thing really hit you hard, huh?

>> *Maaare, sí.*
> Damn straight.

Frustrated? Maare works for that too.

>> *¿Maare, no entiendes?*
> Geez, don't you get it?

madre (*MAH-dreh*) NOUN—Usually reserved for May 10 salutations; *madre* is mother, of course. But in Mexico, and increasingly in the Yucatan by assimilation, *madre* and its plural, *madres*, is very versatile in not very polite conversation. Use it when angry and to impress your new friends. Do not use it in mixed company, at least not initially.

>> *Me vale madre(s).*
> I couldn't care less/give a shit.

▶▶ *Te voy a dar en la madre.*
I'm going to beat you to a pulp.

▶▶ *El camión nos dió en la madre.*
The bus hit our car and there has been significant damage.

▶▶ *¡Ni madres!*
No way!

madrazo (*mah-DRAH-soh*)—also a NOUN, related to the previous motherly entry. A *madrazo* is a hit, a beating, a crash, a large dent in your car's fender, a sudden depletion of your bank account, a roulette dealer taking all your chips, a knock on the head . . . you get the idea.

majar (*mah-HAHR*) VERB—To get hit by something or have one of your extremities flattened. You can hear it used when you are downtown or perhaps at the local clinic.

▶▶ *¡Cuidado niño! ¡Te va a majar el camión!*
Careful kid (as in son or daughter who has ventured out onto the street), you're gonna get hit by a bus!

▶▶ *¿Qué te pasó?*
What happened to you?

▶▶ *Me majé el dedo con la puerta.*
I caught my finger in the door.

Malboro (*mahl-BORE-roh*) SMOKY NOUN—This is the way you say Marlboro, as in the cigarette. don't even attempt, like I stupidly did for the longest time, to pronounce that first *r*; here in Mexico it's called *MAL* (as in bad for you) *boro*. Much easier, don't you think?

malecón (*mah-leh-CON*) NOUN—When the Yucatecans go to Progreso for their *temporada* (SEE *temporada*) many of them will, at some point, visit the *malecón*, which is the boardwalk-like promenade along the shore. During summer and at Easter break, this ocean-front street is converted into one giant cantina. It has been redesigned with a nautical motif and the authorities are very proud of it. Meanwhile, in neighbouring Campeche state, the *Campechanos* are justifiably very proud of their *malecón*, which, stretching along almost the entire waterfront of their port city, is much longer, far more attractive and infinitely more inviting for families, joggers, and bikers and makes the Progreso version look rather insignificant.

mamar *(mah-MAHR)* SUCKY VERB—The word means "to suck," as in a baby on mommy's breast. *Mama* (not *Mamá*) is a female breast, after all. Here in the Yucatan *mamar* also means to get drunk. Imagine the the surprise on the face of the businessman from Mexico City who has just finalized an important business deal with his Yucatecan counterpart who exclaims, in a celebratory manner: "¡*Ahora bien, vamos a mamarnos!*" ("Great! Let's go suck each other!) which of course really means "let's go celebrate with some drinks." Variations on the word are diverse and very versatile and include:

▶ *Estoy bien mamado.*
I am really drunk.

and they are not exclusive to sucking and drinking:

▶ *Estas mamado.*
You are really beefed up (as in you have been working out).

The word can also be used to describe a self-important person who is a pretentious jerk. Not a polite term, so choose your audience carefully.

▶ *No seas mamon.*
Don't be an asshole.

And of course the sexual connotation:

▶ *Mamada*
oral sex on a man

maricón *(mah-ree-CON)* NOUN—A homosexual male. You've probably learned this one from movies featuring latinos. A *maricón* is a fairy, and can also be used to belittle any boy who should dare to shed a tear. *No seas maricón!* will be the stern reprimand from the father (and even sometime the mother) figure who only wants what's best for the boy. ¡*No seas maricón!* will also be used if someone is chickening out of something really macho, like not accompanying the boys to Heladios for beers at noon, when he knows that wife/girlfriend will get upset. Variations include:

▶ *mariconada*
A chickenshit thing.

▶ *marica*
Means the same thing; pronounced *ma-REE-cuh*.

▶ *marimacha*
Another derogative term, this one for the *lesbiana*.

maquiladora (*mah-kee-la-DOH-rah*) NOUN—*Maquiladoras* are large factory-type enterprises where raw materials (imported from abroad) are turned into something useful by Yucatecan labor and then exported back out of the country. *Maquiladoras* are found throughout Mexico but Yucatan has quite a few, so the term may pop up now and again. It's a form of prostitution, but for labor rather than for sex.

Some doubt exists as to the actual benefits of *maquiladoras* to the local economy, since many concessions are made to bring them in in the first place, none of the products reach the local markets, and the employees are nothing more than a pair of hands with not much in the way of career development in the offing. *Maquiladoras* are hated by many locals (especially among the well-off female population) since these new options for employment are located close to villages and towns that have traditionally supplied Merida with a generous stock of maids, gardeners, chauffeurs, thereby resulting in a drastic shortage of same. At the time of this revision, many *maquiladoras* have left the Yucatan and moved eastward. One of the biggest companies still in the state is Lee (jeans), which has a large operation here.

mene mene (*MEH-neh MEH-neh*) EXPRESSION—This comes from *viene viene* and is used by those helpful little old men in greying white guayaberas, dark polyester pants and old sandals, swinging red rags, who can be found anywhere cars are parked, whether it's a supermarket parking lot or a busy section of the street in front of the taqueria of the moment. You are looking in your mirror to see if there is traffic; there is none, just the old guy swinging the rag, yelling *"mene mene"* indicating to you that the coast is clear. Please be aware, however, that not only are these a prime example of Mexico's pitiful old-age retirement options, but they are also not insured and report to no one, should you suffer an accident as a result of an incorrect traffic *mene mene* diagnosis (i.e. oops, there was a car coming after all).

mengano (*men-GAH-noh*) ALTERNATE GENERIC NOUN—Close cousin to *fulano*; *mengano* never leaves without him. (SEE *fulano* for usage.)

mentecato (*men-the-CAH-toh*) SLIMY NOUN—Female: *mentecata*. Originally, this word as *mentecapto* simply means dumb, or lacking in brain power, coming as it does from the latin roots *mente captus* (lacking in mind). In the Yucatan, however, it means a slippery politician, a greedy businessman with little or no scruples in obtaining a profit, a backstabbing neighbour; in general, any person who is simply crooked and evil can fall into the *mentecato* category. Also applied to misbehaving children, the term is used mostly by older folks; nowadays younger people use more explicit terminology. If you are under 30, don't bother using this word; it will make you look antiquated.

▶▶ *¡Mentecato chiquito! ¡No me hace caso!*
That damn kid won't listen to me!

▶▶ *Don Francisco es un mentecato; no me devuelve mi podadora.*
Don Francisco is a jerk; he won't return my lawnmower.

mica (*MEE-cah*) NOUN—A little plastic card or stamp that appeared in or was attached to your Mexican passport. Before the advent of the newest post 9-11 visa, it was a highly desirable accoutrement to your travel arsenal, since it was practically a free pass to enter the Hallowed Land of the Gringo, where many locals like to shop in *Jiustom* (SEE *Jiustom*) and visit the Rat in Orlando etc. etc. The *mica* was obtainable from the U.S. Consulate here in sunny Merida, where you can now pay to set up an appointment and then, at a later date, subject yourself to a potentially hostile interrogation by a jaded U.S. government employee on a power trip.

Mickey (*MEE-kay*) NAME—What the locals call the mouse in Orlando.

miel (*MEEYELL*) NOUN—What you pour on your hotcakes in the morning. *Miel* is actually honey, and the correct term for the sickly sweet artificially flavoured crap would be *jarabe* or syrup, but here it's just *miel*. If you want honey, ask for *miel de abeja*. Bee syrup, if you will. Yucatan is known worldwide for its quality honey, which is made from the Dzidzilché tree, among others, and exported to many countries including Germany. One enterprising businessman started diluting his bee honey with sugar syrup, thereby subjecting the Yucatecan honey to greater scrutiny and nailing yet another coffin in Mexico's reputation as a serious place to do business.

modelo (*moh-DELL-oh*) NOUN—Besides being the name of one of Merida's oldest schools, and the name of a line of beers, the term *modelo* has an interesting meaning when it comes to the sale of your vehicle. It refers to the year of your car, as in: *Se vende Ford modelo 1991*. If someone asks *¿Qué modelo es tu auto?*, you don't say *Es un Falcon*, you say *Es del '87*

modular (*moh-doo-LAHR*) NOUN—This is what the locals call those small stereos where there is one big box that contains the CD player, tape deck, and radio, usually with detachable speakers. Everybody has got a *modular* and a video. The latter has been replaced by the more popular *debedé*, as video cassettes are pretty well obsolete and pirate DVDs are so easy to buy.

montón (*mohn-TOHN*) NOUN—A pile. *Montón* is used when something is expensive or when there is a lot of something, as these examples will illustrate:

▶ *Hay un montón de waches en Mérida.*
There are a lot of people from Mexico City in Merida.

▶ *¿Verdad que hay calor?*
Hot, isn't it?

▶ *Maaare sí, un montón.*
Sure is. Real hot.

▶ *¿Crees que vale 1,000 pesos?*
Do you think it's worth 1,000 pesos?

▶ *No hombre, es un montón de dinero.*
No way, that's too much.

▶ *¿Has ido a Miami?*
Have you been to Miami?

▶ *Sí. Un montón de veces*
Yup, lots of times.

▶ *Un montón de gente*
Lots of people

The most humorous use of the word was in a conversation the other day with a gardener who was describing the police patrols along the highway to his pueblo. He said there were *patrullas* and *anti-montónes*. This is a decomposition of the term *anti-motines*, which could be literally translated as a riot control unit.

mordida (*more-DEE-dah*) NOUN—Literally: the bite. A term universal in all of Mexico, this refers to what happens when the policeman pulls you over for some invented or actual infraction and you suggestively ask if there is a way to pay the fine now, as opposed to having your car impounded and getting a ticket. Policemen do not like to write tickets and will play along eagerly in most cases; sometimes they will offer to take that fine for you as a convenience to you, the time-strapped citizen. Initially they may feign indignation at being asked about paying a fine; this is only temporary and part of the theatrics.

Caveat emptor: In the case of Federal Highway Police (those snappy black cars and the policemen—straight out of a Mexican '70s cops-and-robbers movie—that patrol federal highways) be very careful with your wording and don't offer if you don't have a substantial sum of cash. Substantial is in the several hundreds. In fact, don't initiate this; you may be arrested. Also used in other situations involving cash-strapped government employees in positions of power. The process of bribing authorities to move things along is known as giving them a *mordida*.

motel (*mo-TELL*) SLEAZY NOUN—The word *motel* in the Yucatan doesn't evoke heart-warming memories of family trips in the station wagon. Instead, say *motel* and any Yucatecan will immediately think prostitutes, affairs and in general illicit sex. That is because all the hotels called motels on the *periférico* (SEE *periférico*) rent rooms by the hour and that is where you go when you are engaging in such activities, which are more common than you might think. Merida motels are sometimes themed, with each room featuring a different ambience you might enjoy, i.e. Egyptian, Roman, jungle, etc. Please note that these observations are not based on any personal experience of this author, but from the photos one can enjoy on a giant, flashing neon advertising sign featuring many rotating ads, strategically positioned for all to see on the Prolongacion Montejo.

mozo (*MO-so*) NOUN—The word doesn't rhyme with Bozo as in the clown, so say it right. In a proper and traditional yucatecan household, there will be several types of service personnel, such as the cook, the laundry person, the nanny, the housekeeper, and a couple of mozos. Nowadays, most people have only a *mozo* or a *muchacha* or maybe both. The *mozo* is the young man of Mayan descent who lives in your house, does the dishes, sweeps and mops, keeps the cars clean, tends to any and all pets and the garden, and sometimes, if you are really lucky, cooks your meals. He is the male version of the *muchacha* (SEE *below*) or acts as a complement to that very important figure in the Yucatecan household.

muchacha (*moo-CHA-cha*) NOUN—A young (very young and getting younger these days) female of Mayan heritage who works in your home, washing, cleaning, doing dishes, cooking, caring for the baby; basically all those things you can't do what with all those coffee breakfast gossip sessions going on. This is what makes living in Merida and in Mexico in general "so great."

For the social-conscious, hearing a child say *mi muchacha* like they were referring to the family pet is tough to swallow.

mulix (*mu-LEESH*) ADJECTIVE—Curly hair. If you are a curly haired person, it's likely that you were given this nickname: *El Mulix Fernández*.

mulix

N

naca (*NAH-kah*) NOUN—A *naca*, (masculine *naco*), is a person of the female sex from the bottom of the socio-economic ladder, commonly defined as having no taste and usually brown in color, with a minimum of discretionary income, or, if an income is available, unable to "correctly" spend his or her money resulting in the purchase of garish furniture/clothing or what-have-you. Despised by all social classes (the upper classes want nothing to do with the *nacos*, and use this term to distance themselves from their countrymen/women while the lower classes aspire not be classified as such.

For many, a person obviously of indigenous background, regardless of education, employment, geographics; is a *naco*, simply because of his indigenous heritage.

Sample usage: *Nos estaba atendiendo una naca, pero UNA NACA*. Note the emphasis in the repetition of the *UNA NACA*, which means that the person telling the story was being looked after by a really indigenous looking person, probably with a gold tooth and really brown skin.

Derivations you will hear of this usually derogatory term include:

▸ *naquito/a*
More derogative than the original, usually spoken accompanied by a dismissive head shaking

▸ *naquiza*
A reference to the whole mass of brown people out there as in "this TV program really appeals to the *naquiza*."

naranja agria (*nah-RAHN-ha AH-gree-ah*) SOUR NOUN—The sour orange is what Yucatecans traditionally use to marinade (often combining it with the red *achiote* paste) chicken or pork, to tenderize and give it flavour, before grilling. *Naranja agria* also makes a great refresco, or water-based fruit drink.

nightclub (*easy pronunciation, huh?*) NOUN—Also spelled NIGTHCLUB, this is the accepted term for strip bars. No jazz or live rock and roll in these places, just strippers, often watered-down alcohol, and dubious activity in the back rooms. You will find these around Merida's beltway, known here as *el periférico*. Note that strip clubs here are more "hands on" than their over-controlled north-of-the-border counterparts.

novela (*no-VEH-la*) NOUN—The nightly soap opera. The two national television networks—TV Azteca and Televisa—pump out a series of idiotic soap operas that reflect *wach* culture in its most asinine form. These programs, along with the rest of the mind-numbing programming coming from the nation's capital, are contributing to the homogenization of Mexican culture (everyone becomes a *wach*) and the decline of any real culture in the country. any real culture in the country. It's an important form of entertainment for folks with nothing better to do and who live vicariously through the exaggerated characters they see on the small screen. Nothing better after a hard day of work than to sit back and watch or gustar (SEE *gustar*) one of the many prime-time novelas. It's not unusual to see kids (especially girls) from age 11 and up addicted to watching episodes featuring such original material as marital deceit and violence, rape, unwanted pregnancies, inter-social class romance and its ramifications, etc., etc.. Pablum for the masses.

Nueba Yor (*nweh-bah-YOR*) CITY NAME—The city where Giuliani once ruled, known in the tongue of Shakespeare as New York.

nylom (*NIE-lom*) NOUN—This is of course, the plastic material known as nylon, as in nylon rope. If you're planning on doing some shopping, especially in the *mercado*, you may want to take along a *bolsa de nylom* (a plastic bag). If Publix or Safeway ever come to town, the cashier will have to ask ¿*papel o nylom?* Another use of the word occurs when it is raining. Your muchacha or mozo will leave for the day and if you ask her or him if he brought an umbrella, he will probably reply that he will be fine; he has his nylom.

O

onda (*oN-dah*) WAVY NOUN—Onda means "wave" as in *micro-onda* or microwave. But when you add the word *que* in front, it becomes a casual greeting:

> ▸ *¿Qué onda?*
> What's up?

oso (*OH-so*) NOUN—Besides the obvious "bear" translation, to "make the bear" (*hacer el oso*) is to do something embarrassing. Especially popular among hyper-self-conscious pre-teen drama queens (at the time of this writing) *hacer el oso* is social suicide.

> ▸ *¡¡Qué OSO!!*
> How EMBARRASSING!!
> —a group of teen girls will shriek in unison, covering their mouths with their hands, wide-eyed and doubling over in laughter.

Oxcutzcab (*osh-coots-CAHB*) TOWN—There were only two entries under the letter O and people (even many Yucatecans themselves) have problems pronouncing this one (SEE ALSO *Dzibilchaltun*), so: two good reasons to include the place in this dictionary. Located near Ticul (SEE ALSO *Ticul*), Oxcutzcab features a great fruit market, as the little town is in the heart of citrus growing country. Take a pickup and load up on plenty of fresh and cheap oranges, AKA *chinas*.

P

pam (*PUM*) NOUN—1) No, it's not a non-stick cooking spray. This is what you buy at the bakery. While most Yucatecans will say *panadería* and *panificadora* (note the *n*) a real *Yuca* will always say *pam* when referring to anything to do with bread. 2) The National Action Party, Partido de Accion Nacional—PAN—political party that overturned the PRI after 70 years of monopolist rule in Mexico at the federal and more recently, state level in Yucatan.

> *Vota por el PAM.*
> Vote for the PAN.

panqué (*pun-KEH*) NOUN—Pancakes are called hotcakes and *panqué* is actually a pan cake i.e. the kind that comes in a loaf pan and is usually pretty plain. Sometimes pecans are added and it is called *panqué de nuez*.

papaya (*pah-PIE-yah*) FRUITY NOUN—You know this is a fruit; there is the big smellier local version and the smaller "Hawaiian" or *Maradol* variety. *Sin embargo*, there is another use for the word. (SEE *queso* in this dictionary for more insight.)

pareja (*pa-REH-ha*) NOUN—Literally: a pair. *Una pareja de idiotas* is a pair of idiots. Used to describe romantic interests as in:

> *¿Fulana todavía no tiene pareja?*
> Fulana doesn't have a boyfriend yet?

Also used in the world of parenting. If you have a daughter; especially if you have "only" a daughter, some members of the *machista* society will disapprove and ask you over and over if you are not going to *buscar la parejita*, or go for the pair.

In the world of household help (SEE *servicio*) the ideal situation would be a couple working for you, as in:

> *¿Ya tienes muchacha?*
> Do you have a maid?

▸▸ *No, fíjate que tengo una pareja.*
No, I have hired a couple (as in *mozo* and *muchacha* tag team).

pasto (*PASS-toh*) NOUN—In Merida, your lawn is called *el pasto*. Other parts of the Spanish-speaking world call it a *cesped*, but *pasto* sounds better in the context of the Mayan heritage. It just rolls off the tongue better.

patan (*pah-TAHN*) NOUN—A jerk. (SEE *mentecato*. Same usage.)

patio (*same as English*) NOUN—While in English this word evokes romantic images of an orderly little area somewhere in the garden, here it is a place where one goes to throw the garbage or perhaps, as is the case in rural areas of Yucatan, where you go to relieve yourself with some ripped up newspaper and a small amount of lime. Pigs and chickens often live in the patios too. There's a whole world back there; all kinds of things happening.

patrón (*pah-TROHM*) NOUN—This, besides being the name of Yucatan's first opposition governor (PAN), is the boss of any household. The female version is the *patrona*. This is a remnant of the "good old" *hacienda* days when the "Indians" knew their place and before the advent of *maquiladoras*. Nowadays, the *muchachas* and the *mozos* and the *jardineros* and the *planchadoras* (SEE *servicio*) work for and preferably respect their *patrón*, who pays them.

It is common in the markets and on the street to have fruit sellers, *tortilla* ladies and parking helpers (the guys swinging the red cloth around that help you in and out of a parking space in exchange for some coinage—SEE *mene mene*) address one as *patron* or *patrona* or even *patroncito*, *cito* being the diminutive form of anything.

pay (*PIE*) NOUN—There is no Spanish word for what we *Norteamericanos* call pie so the word is the same, only spelled differently. Sometimes. You will see the on the menu *pie de manzana* which technically means "apple foot," or perhaps you will see *pay de manzana* which would be the more "correct" version.

pay

pedo (*PEH-doe*) NOUN—A fart. But modern SLANG has enhanced and diversified its meaning. Not all applications are Yucatecan by any means, but all are heard extremely frequently. Take note of the following applications to get an idea of the versatility of the fart word:

» *Me eché un pedo.*
I farted (traditional meaning).

» *¿Que pedo?*
What's up? (As a greeting.)

» *Es un pedo.*
It's a hassle (as a description of a problem).

» *Traigo un pedo.*
I have a problem (idem).

» *Estoy pedo.*
I am drunk.

» *una peda*
a drinking binge

» *Es tu pedo.*
It's your problema.

» *Se metió en un pedo.*
He got himself into a spot of trouble.

pegar (*peh-GAHR*) VERB—To hit; also to stick together. *Pegamento* is glue, hence the sticky definition. Check out these examples:

» *Nos pegó duro el huracam.*
The hurricane hit us hard.

» *¡Pégalo!*
Hit him!

» *Pégate a ella.*
Go and stand next to her.

» *Y no te desprendes de ella.*
And don't leave her side

» *Tiene su pegue.*
He is popular, girls like to be around him.

» *Estábamos pegaditos a la pared.*
We were right up next to the wall.

» *Esa blusa no pega.*

That blouse doesn't match your outfit.

pelaná (*pell-ah-NAH*) VULGARITY—The Mayan term *pel'aná*, heard among those of obvious Mayan ancestry, literally means "your mothers' privates," and is not at all socially acceptable. In a heated cantina argument, if you wanted to bring the tone up a notch, you might shout at your adversary *"pel'ana!"* and that should heat things up nicely. Don't believe your newfound friends at the cantina when they insist that this means something nice and you should say it to the big rough-looking character at the bar.

pena ajena (*PEH-nah ah-HEH-nah*) STATE OF MIND—That uncomfortable feeling you get when seeing someone do something embarrassing. Yucatecans, much like people all over the world, are very conscious of "fitting in" with what their society deems as "correct" and anything seen as falling outside those strict canons of acceptable behavior, is seen with a feeling of *pena ajena*.

Be aware that your position as a foreigner relieves you of much of this social pressure and anything weird you may do (dress inappropriately, say inappropriate things, talk to stray animals in the street) will be attributed to your foreignness and will not cause anyone to feel *pena ajena*.

pendejo (*pen-DEH-ho*) an extremely popular VULGARITY, increasingly used in everyday conversation. A *pendejo* is someone stupid, someone who is constantly screwing up due to their own incompetence, someone who doesn't see what is really happening around them. The female version is equally popular, used among women to describe the less intelligent members of their sex. While *pendejo* and *pendeja* are used by women in their descriptions of men and women, it is rare to hear a man say that a certain woman is a *pendeja*, unless of course they are an ex-couple and she is insisting on child support payments. But for the most part, they are still ladies, after all.

Many variations of the term exist:

» *pendejez*
stupidity

» *Cuando se le quite la pendejez...*
When the stupidity wears off...

> *pendejear*
> to go around being a *pendejo*, walking around in a trance

> *pendejadas*
> stupid things or statements

> *No digas pendejadas.*
> Don't say such idiotic things.

perech (*peh-RECH*) MAYAN ADJECTIVE—A couple of examples will illustrate the meaning of this extremely common word; no one uses the Spanish equivalents, except those *waches*, who after being here a short while quickly adopt the Mayan terminology.

> *Llegamos perech.*
> We made it just in time.

> *Estuvo perech la comida.*
> We almost ran out of food.

> *Estamos pereches de gasolina.*
> Our gas is getting a little low.

periférico (*peh-ree-FEHR-ee-coh*) NOUN—The beltway, or ring road. Once a very narrow four-lane highway, two lanes in either direction separated by a green belt, that completely encircles the city of Merida, the *periférico* has become a modern six-lane highway. The center green belt remains, but the rest is all modernity. Three lanes in either direction, wide shoulders, on ramps, off ramps, over and underpasses. Many locals like to use it as their personal race track and the state police have a field day issuing speeding tickets.

Many hotels of ill-repute and nightclubs are located along the *periférico* and nighttime driving used to be dangerous at times, what with drunken drivers, stalled unlit trucks, bicycles appearing out of nowhere, *policías* looking to fatten the kitty with a *mordida*, etc. However, while the hotels and nightclubs are still there, the driving safety situation has improved enormously with the new, modern highway.

pikza (*PEEK-sah*) NOUN—This is what some people call that enormously popular Italian food item commercialized so successfully by Domino's and Pizza Hut. Merida's best *pikza* is Boston's Pizza for thick crusts and inventive ingredient combinations and Rafaello's for thin-crust, wood oven baked deliciousness, in my humble opinion.

pirata (*pee-RAH-tah*) NOUN—Pirate. In Mexico there is pirated version of everything, from clothing brands to DVDs to software and the Yucatan is no exception. A stroll downtown or a lunch on the beach in Progreso will quickly make this very clear. I think we're right up there with China.

pirix (*pee-REESH*) NOUN—This word will almost certainly be another of the first your new Yucatecan friends will teach you and howl outrageously at when you utter it in polite company. Considered offensive, it literally means "anus" but everyone uses it as a general term for the entire area immediately below where your backbone ends *(SEE bobox)* The most common variant of this word is in the expression *tu pirix* which translates as "your ass," which is a popular comeback if you say something that could be considered a teasing insult. Don't pay attention to your charming new friends at the cantina; do NOT say this in front of anyone to whom you will be applying a job later, or that pretty girl in the corner (although a pretty girl in a Merida cantina would be a rare sight, indeed).

playa

playa (*PLY-yah*)—Beach. Yucatecans take to the beach during *Semana Santa* (Easter Break) and the summer holidays, which they call *la temporada* *(SEE temporada)*. Snowbirds from Canada and the frigid U.S. now visit the beaches as well, during those times of the year when snow is common where they are from and the beach houses are empty.

Popular destinations on the playa include:

▸ **Progreso** (*pro-GREH-so*)—The main port for the state and the original beach destination for most Yucatecans and visitors during the summer months. Cruise ships run by Ships operated by Carnival Cruise Lines dock here on Mondays and occasionally Wednesdays or Thursdays, disgorging hundreds of well-fed, white sneaker-ed Americans from the south who wander aimlessly along the *malecón* (SEE *malecón*) and wonder why the cruise ship stopped here. During summer vacations the town becomes one giant cantina.

▸ **Chicxulub** (*chick-shoe-LOOB*)—Once the place for Merida's well-to-do summer vacationers, Chicxulub is now a popular place for snowbirds who rent houses over the winter, and the well-to-do have moved further along.

▸ **Uaymitun** (*why-mee-TOON*)—This is where the well-to-do have moved to, as well as points further along the highway. Not a town per se, but an area. There is a flamingo observatory tower you can climb and occasionally spot some of the pink birds.

▸ **Telchac** (*tell-CHUCK*)—The more adventurous of the well-to-do as well as some foreigners, live way out here. The town is the last little spot of civilization before points further out, like San Bruno, San Crisanto, and the like.

▸ **Chelem** and **Chuburna** (*cheh-LEHM* and *choo-boor-NAH*)—These are two towns left of Progreso when coming from Merida and are home to the middle- and lower-middle-class Yucatecans, who also want to enjoy beach life during the hot months of July and August and during Easter break. Houses here are more modest and there is an increasing number of Canadians and Americans who are buying property here, as it is much cheaper than on the Chicxulub side.

playar (*ply-YAHR*) BEACH VERB—If you took this literally it would mean "to beach," but of course nothing is that literal. This is a popular summer activity, or was, before people started bringing televisions and Nintendos and Xboxes to the beach. In July and August, everyone moves to the beach (SEE *temporada*) and taking a walk in the afternoon with your friends, girlfriends, cousins, etc., was the thing to do. Put on a wrap or some shorts and away you go, often walking miles before

THE MODERN YUCATAN DICTIONARY

turning back. Enjoying the sunset and good conversation was the point of this exercise, something we all could use a little more of these days.

Price (*PRICE*) PLACE NAME—The locals used to call Costco this, since when they opened they were called Price Club. The merger with Costco to become Price Club-Costco and then simply Costco, went unnoticed by Yucatecans who continued to call the store Price. It's really pronounced *priiiiice*, by the way. At the time of this writing, the Price reference has faded away and now it's *Cosco* (without the *t*).

pueblo (*PWEH-blow*) NOUN—Small town or village, source of domestic help for Merida's overworked housewives. *Mentalidad de pueblo* means "small-town mentality."

puta (*POOH-tah*) NOUN—1) Derogative term for a "loose" woman. In the Merida of Fernando Espejo's memory, a loose woman would be one who dared to leave home before getting married or who went on a date without a *chaperón* (SEE *chaperón*). Thankfully some of these backward traditions have disappeared; a development lamented by Merida's elderly citizens and probably celebrated by the girls of today.

2) A violent expression of disappointment or anger. Your bank calls to tell you that your account is overdrawn; you hang up and shake your head and say ¡*puta!* Not socially acceptable unless you are with a group of same-sex acquaintances and there is a certain degree of *confianza*.

puta madre (*POOH-tah MAH-dreh*)—Expression of anger and often disbelief, the intensity of which is established by the tone and volume used when uttering this expression. *Puta*—whore; *madre*—mother. Not nice and not at all socially accepted; I wouldn't recommend trying it out on anyone during your first visit to Merida. In a polite society, however, there are always other ways to say the same thing without actually saying it. The popular Yucatecan expression *ta mare* is based on the vulgar original, as is *pa su mecha* (perhaps not Yucatecan), *puchi vida* or simply *puchi* (pronounced *poochy*), and a host of others. The original version can be used, once you have the pronunciation down and feel comfortable descending to this level, among groups of men who know each other and the ice has been broken, so to speak. Never use in the presence of a female, no matter how liberated she claims to be or how filthy her vocabulary. She still considers herself a lady, even if you no longer share that appreciation.

puto (*POOH-toh*) NOUN—Another derogative term, this time applied to any male who displays feminine qualities or is gay. Also applied to male prostitutes. If you accidentally use this as an expression of anger *a la puta*, you are definitely giving yourself away as a gringo.

Q

queso (*KEH-soh*) NOUN—Cheese. Please be aware that in the way that *chile* has a double meaning in that it also means the male sex organ, *queso* refers to the female sex organ. Its usage in this way is almost exclusively the domain of the men, although there are women who enjoy the occasional joke with the hidden or implied connotations, although never in mixed company unless there is a high degree of *confianza*. You would have to be very careful who you are speaking with if you open your refrigerator and innocently announce to the bystanders that your cheese smells funny. (SEE *papaya*)

quiebra (*kih-EH-brah*) BREAKING VERB—"*¡Quiebra, quiebra, quiebra!*" is what the *mene mene* man (SEE *mene mene*) will shout as you are struggling into, or maneuvering out of, a parallel parking situation, meaning that you need to turn your wheels in whatever direction his red flannel rag is waving.

quitar (*kih-TAHR*) VERB—"Take away" is the generally accepted Spanish meaning of this word. In Merida, again, in addition to the norm, a different usage is common. It becomes to leave. The verb becomes reflexive and acquires new applications that are inherently Yucatecan—classics if you will. If you are leaving a party you might say:

▶▶ *'Ta bueno, me voy.*
Well, I'm leaving.

To which your host or other party guests may reply:

▶▶ *¿Por qué te quitas tan temprano?*
Why are you leaving so soon?

▶▶ *Es que se gastaron las chevas; y tengo que chambear mañana.*
Well, there's no more beer, and I have to work tomorrow.

If you weren't able to attend, you might run into someone from the revelry the night before and ask them:

>> *¿Cómo se puso la fiesta?*
   How (did the party put itself) was the party?

and get this reply:

>> *No sé. Me quité temprano*
   I don't know, I left early

Other uses could be:

>> *¡Quítate!*
   Get out of the way!

>> *¿A qué hora te vas a quitar?*
   What time are you leaving?

Quitar is something you will hear a lot in Yucatan.

quiúbole (*key-OO-boh-leh*) WACH EXPRESSION—This is not Yucatecan; rather it is SLANG from Mexico City, land of the *waches* who, along with their television and their *tacos al pastor*, have inserted themselves pervasively into every culture they can get their tentacles into. You will hear this term now in the formerly "White City."

R

rackets (*RA-kets*) NOUN—This is an abomination of the English word racks, as in shelving. There is a local company that advertises its services as *Closets y Rackets*. Kind of funny, if you ask me; what do they do—come to your house and install a closet and make a lot of noise? Maybe just plain old "racks" was too difficult to pronounce.

redrogear (*reh-droh-heh-AHR*)—An old Spanish word, long since abandoned in other parts of the Spanish-speaking world, that is used by older people to denote careful perusal, usually of a place. If you are in a junk or second-hand shop, looking around, or in a supermarket, taking your time to check out every new and imported food item that has reached the shelves, you are *redrogeando*. You can also *redrogear* in your underwear drawer, if you think there might be something interesting stored there.

relaciones (*reh-lah-SEEOH-nehs*) NOUN—Relations, commonly used to primly and prudishly describe a sexual relationship, without mentioning that taboo word, sex.

> ▶▶ *¿Ya tuvistes relaciones?*
> Did you have sex?

remate (*reh-MAH-teh*) FINALIZING NOUN—The term *remate* comes from the verb *rematar*: to finish something (or someone). If you are at a store and there is a sign that says *remate* along with a large pile of really ugly clothes, say, that means the stuff is being liquidated.

Alternatively, to *rematar* someone is to off them. Kill them, in other words.

In Merida, *remate* also is the name of the beginning of the Paseo de Montejo. For some reason someone started calling it *El Remate* (the end) when it is really the beginning, of the magnificent Paseo de Montejo. While there is occasionally some debate about the correctness of the term, the name stuck and when you tell your Yucatecan friends *nos vemos en el Remate* they will immediately know where you will be.

retentado (*reh-ten-TAH-doe*) ADJECTIVE—This is one of those old Spanish words that has survived the passage of time in the Yucatan thanks to 400 years of isolation from the rest of Mexico and is used when describing the severity of a condition, such as when you are suffering from a severe case of allergies when you might exclaim:

▶ *Está retentada mi alergia hoy.*
Today my allergy is really acting up.

If you are having a prolonged coughing fit, you might explain:

▶ *'Toy retentado de la tos.*
My cough is really acting up.

If you are in a bad mood, you might hear someone say (about you):

▶ *Ni le hables, tiene retentado su wá.*
Don't bother talking to him, he's all grumpy.

S

sabor (*suh-BORE*) NOUN—The usual meaning is taste or flavour; as in:

▸ *Tiene buen sabor.*
  Has a good taste/is tasty.

Although more common several years ago, one can still hear the question ¿*Coca o sabor?* when you ask for a *refresco* (soda pop) at a restaurant or a party. Amazingly, if you reply *sabor*, the waiter doesn't pursue the matter any further and brings whatever flavour he comes across; nor do the people around you ask for any specific flavour; they simply ask for *sabor*.

sabucam (*suh-boo-KAHM*) BAGGY NOUN— To go to the market without your trusty plaid *sabucan* (spelled with an *n* and pronounced with an *m*) is just crazy. Where are you going to put those avocados and that half pound of fresh leg of pork?

One thing middle to lower socio-economic class Yucatecans have been doing for decades—and something you might well adopt—is taking their bags with them when they go shopping, thereby preventing the profusion of plastic so common these days. While most North American markets have fairly recently begun to promote and sell their re-usable and "green" shopping bags (which you always tend to forget to bring to the store) Yucatecans have been doing this for years.

sabucam

sacudir (*sah-koo-DEER*) VERB—To shake. While shaking your sofa or your table may seem difficult if not downright impossible, it would appear that this is what Yucatecans are doing (or at least their *muchachas* are anyway) with their furniture. Actually, here it means to dust off or clean. So if someone tells you *sacude la mesa*, don't start lifting and shaking, simply grab a cloth and remove the crumbs from breakfast, and maybe give it a wipe down with a damp Magitel cloth.

Saga (*SAH-gah*)—Apparently, far from being a long, incredibly rich tale filled with outrageous characters performing heroic feats in exotic locales, this was also the name of a brand of t-shirts that was popular in the Yucatan for a time.

Saga

T-shirts, like undershirts, were (and are still in many cases) worn under the dress shirt; usually a *guayabera*, to protect it from the inevitable sweating that occurs during the course of the day. Like Kleenex did for paper tissue, Saga became the generic name for the t-shirt in many Yucatecan households:

- *¿Te pusistes tu Saga?*
  Did you put on your t-shirt/undershirt?

or this classic uttered by some household help:

- *¿Aliso la Saga?*
  Do I smooth the shirts? (SEE *alisar*)

I only mention this because it is still possible in the Yucatan to hear someone say *Saga* for a t-shirt. Since the author of this dictionary sells t-shirts on the side, a young man (late teens) recently asked at a fair:

- *¿A cómo la Saga?*
  How much for the shirts?

sarandear (*sah-ran-deh-AHR*) VERB—Yet another antique Castillian term you won't learn in Spanish classes these days. The way I understand it, the word means to shake. As in:

- *Tuve que sarandear esos niños para que reaccionen.*
  I had to give those kids a shake to get their attention.

- *Nos dimos una sarandeada en esa carretera.*
  That (bumpy) highway really shook us up

secre (*SEH-creh*) NOUN/PROFESSION— This is similar to the idea of the *chalan* (SEE *chalán*). Similar usage, functions, and responsibilities but perhaps more along the lines of an assistant rather than just a worker you can order around (although you will) and comes from the word *secretaría*, or secretary.

separar (*seh-par-RAHR*) VERB—To separate; as in

▶ *Separa esos que siempre se andan peleando.*
Split those ones up; they're always fighting.

In Merida, *separar* has another, more local meaning and usage: Set aside. If you go by a toy store at Christmas time, you will see signs telling you *separa sus juguetes,* which does not mean that your toys might be combined with someone else's and this is a bad thing; it means that you can set aside the toys you want to buy for Christmas and pay for them little by little.

servicio (*sir-VISS-ee-oh*) NOUN—A generic term for all household help, including *el mozo, la muchacha, la nana, la cocinera, la lavandera, la planchadora, el jardinero, el chofer, el* . . . do I have to go on? It's amazing how many Yucatecans still like to believe that they really need to have a muchacha tagging along at the mall, in the restaurant, or even on holidays, looking after the kids. Are the kids really that much of a bother? Also amazing is how young the modern *muchacha* is; often the girl taking care of the baby doesn't look much older than 12 or 13.

shores (*SHOH-rez*) TWO-SYLLABLE NOUN—This is painted on the wall of a clothing store downtown and although by itself you could never figure it out, when read in the context of the rest of the junk painted haphazardly on the wall (*t-shirts, vestidos, blusas*) you realize that this it the word for *pantalones cortos* or short pants: shorts.

si (*SEE*) AFFIRMATIVE—Everyone knows this word! But in Merida, when you invite someone to your home for a dinner or party or a meeting, it can also mean *no. Si* means "I heard you and I may even show up at your house but then again I have to keep my options open and can't commit to anything so maybe I won't be there after all and I certainly don't want to hurt your feelings or look bad in your eyes thanks for asking me but I just don't know." Just saying "yes" is a simple way to avoid explanations regarding whether or not you are going to accept, although admittedly it does infuriate your new-to-Merida host when he or she realizes that he has cooked for eighteen and only seven show up.

siecierto (*see-ehss-SEE-YAYR-toh*)—Another form of AFFIRMATION; used when you tell someone something that he or she had not realized or thought about before and, realizing that it is true what you have said, will utter with a slow nodding of their head, *¡siecierto!* It is the contracted version of *sí es cierto*, which is the conversational equivalent of the English "true."

siempre (*see-EM-preh*)—Usually means always. But locally, it is used as a kind of "still" or "after all." See the following examples to better understand the quirky usage of the word

>> *Siempre vienen.*
They are always coming *or* they are coming after all.
(As in a band or circus that had originally announced their decision not to come.)

>> *Siempre si voy a ir.*
I am going after all.

>> *¿Siempre no fueron?*
They (or you) didn't go after all?

sirviente/a (*sir-vee-EN-teh/tah*) NOUN—Merida must be one of the few privileged places in the world where, up until a few years ago, you could still open up the classifieds section of the local paper and find an ad for servants. Servants!

sisal (*see-SAHL*) NOUN—What people in Europe and the U.S. called the henequén (SEE *henequén*) when it arrived in bales off ships that sailed from Yucatan's main port at the time, Sisal. Sisal was destroyed many moons ago by a hurricane and has never recovered. Progreso was built, as it was closer to Merida, and the factories processing the henequén fibre and is, of course, now the Yucatan's main port.

smoking (*duh*) NOUN—The term used for a tuxedo. Probably comes from that Bond-era term "smoking jacket," when men were men and wore these penguin suits while enjoying a cigar in the so-called drawing room. Since there seems to be some sort of speech impediment that prevents a great majority of the world's Spanish-speaking population from pronouncing the letter *s* at the beginning of a word, they insert an *e* to make it easier, thus *smoking* becomes *esmokin* or, better yet, *esmokim*. (SEE ALSO *eskai* for another example of this, and *etiqueta* for more on dressing up.)

Smoking Club #2 PLACE—The "Smoking" in the name of this popular Merida eatery located at the San Fernando glorieta or roundabout refers to the *smoking* as defined above, and is not, as some people first suspect upon reading the sign, a club for Marlboro addicts.

solicitar (*so-lih-sih-TAHR*) APPLICATION VERB—*Solicitar* means "to apply for." The *solicitud* is the application, *solicitud de trabajo*, the job application. If you are looking for someone to come and work for you, you are *solicitando*. A funny application of this term was heard in my store recently, where I had posted the sign *Solicito Empleada*. The young man (he obviously couldn't read the *empleadA* part) asked me "Ya solicitarom?" by which he meant to ask me if I had found the employee I had been *solicitando*.

super (*SOO-pehr*) SHOPPING NOUN—If you are going to go grocery shopping you can either hit the market for some push-comes-to-shove activity or visit a supermarket, known here as *el super*. There are several major chains to choose from at the moment, but of course this could change. Here's a short list of the major players:

>> **San Francisco** —AKA *San Pancho*—The eminent local chain that was once king of supermarkets, run by the Abraham family who also run the rather dilapidated 7-11 franchise for the peninsula. For decades they were the only game in town and had the power to prevent chains from coming from the D.F. Now they have been eclipsed by both Mexican and foreign companies and only die-hard *Yucas* shop there.

>> **Carrefour** —The French chain came to town, built a giant store near the convention center, had some limited success, then sold all their Latin American or at least Mexican holdings. Their store is now a Chedraui.

>> **Chedraui** —AKA *Chedrauli*—One of the first non-Yucatecan supermarket chains to break into the Yucatecan market, this company whose name is the last name of its owner, first moved into the plaza by the Monumento a la Patria on Paseo de Montejo. When they opened, people flocked from all around to buy their Gruyere and other great cheeses, previously unavailable in the formerly "White City."

>> **Walmart** —AKA *GualWar*—Nothing I can say about this except that it is clean, very competitive and offers covered parking which always impresses our visitors from the U.S. or Canada.

THE MODERN YUCATAN DICTIONARY

▸ **Superama** —A Walmart company with an identity crisis. They came in promising to be an upscale experience with specialty food, personalized attention and prices a little higher than the rest. Now they still have the reputation and the products, but are competing on price and the service generally is on par with any other supermarket—not great.

▸ **Comercial Mexicana** AKA *La Comer*—This giant company comes out of Mexico City and is a monster. They have two versions; regular and super-sized i.e. Mega. They are affiliated with Costco in Mexico.

▸ **Costco** and **Sam's Club** —The two membership-only grocery and Chinese-merchandise mega stores compete with each other. Costco is geared more towards a pleasant experience with good service, good products, and many deli items. Sams is a more commercial experience, with weary, overworked employees who are not real friendly, and their emphasis is more towards small mom-and-pop stores. They made an effort and try to compete with Costco with the specialty foods and even installed a bakery (like Costco) but there is no comparison.

T

'ta bueno (*tuh-BWAY-no*) EXPRESSION OF AFFIRMATION—A shortened form of *está bueno* used instead of the probably more correct *está bien* or *'ta bien*. When someone tells you something and you understand, you reply this. If used as a question; say, in the restaurant buffet line when you ask the chef or cook ¿*'ta bueno?* it obviously means "is that good?" You will also hear this used as an expression of incredulous disbelief; someone is telling someone else about how he or she did this or that and the person hearing the story can't believe it, the person will say to the one telling the tale "*aha . . . 'ta bueno*" or "*eeeeeeehhhhh 'ta bueno.*" Often shortened to simply "*eeeeehhhh.*" A reader has pointed out that the *'ta bueno*, in the case of expressing incredulity, is sometimes followed by *tu*, becoming, *ta bueno, tu,* which gives the statement a little more punch.

técnico (*TECK-nih-coh*) NOUN—Professional kind of person, almost exclusively male, who you call when there is a problem with your computer.

▸ *No funciona Windows, jefe.*
  Windows is on the fritz, boss.

▸ *Llama al técnico.*
  Call the tech guy.

TelCel (*tell-CELL*) COMMUNICATIVE NOUN—Mexico's cellular phone quasi-monopoly. You will see their ads before enjoying a movie at the local *cine* (SEE *cine*) where white people specially selected to represent the Mexican ideal will frolic happily knowing that "*todo México es territorio TelCel*" (all of Mexico is *TelCel* territory) which of course is a blatant overstatement. There are other companies such as *Iusacell* (simply called *Iusa* in the locals' never-ending insistence on shortening anything with three syllables or more to two) and *Axtel*, but these are marginal and coverage is spotty.

tele (*TELL-leh*) NOUN—Short for television, as in

> *'Toy gustando tele.*
> I'm watching TV.

teléfono (*teh-LEH-foh-no*) NOUN—A phone. Also used as the abbreviated term for telephone number. No one says *número de teléfono*; it's far too long, so save yourself the trouble and don't even try it. People will ask you for your *teléfono*, in which case you are expected to give them your phone number; don't hand over the actual device.

TelMex (*TELL-MEX*) NOUN—The national telephone monopoly. Not Yucatecan, but it always comes up in daily conversations. Their service has improved somewhat over the years I have been here, but it is still the only game in town for telephone service and you have to jump through their hoops if you want to play.

temporada (*tem-por-RAH-da*) NOUN—The usual Spanish meaning for this word is "season," and it is used that way in Merida as well, as in:

> *Es temporada de canicas/mangos/beisbol.*
> It's marble/mango/baseball season.

But the most usual meaning of the word, when someone says *La Temporada*, he or she refers to the two month summer vacations when everyone and their offspring and those horrible relatives from Campeche (*ni modo que les digamos que no vengam*) go to the beach on the shores of the Gulf of Mexico.

tener (*teh-NAIR*) VERB—The usage of the verb *tener* in the Yucatan, especially in villages where Mayan has not yet been eradicated by the devastating cultural monolith that is the television, can prove challenging at first. Apparently this comes from Mayan grammar having been applied to Spanish. Here are some examples, first in regular Spanish, followed by English and then Yucatecan village Spanish:

> *Lo he visto.*
> I have seen it/him.
> *Lo tengo visto.*

> *Fui a Merida.*
> I went to Merida.
> *Tengo ido en Mérida.*

>> *Se lo di.*
I gave it to him.
Se lo tengo dado.

Ticul *(tee-COOL)* TOWN—The town of Ticul is in this dictionary just because I was writing about Oxcutzcab and mentioned Ticul *(SEE Oxcutzcab)*. Ticul is famous for its shoes which are plentiful, inexpensive, and extremely popular with the local ladies, although it isn't Jimmy Choo if you know what I mean. It is also known for its clay pots, frogs, and other decorative items for your home, as well as being the home of the unfortunately no longer recommendable Los Almendros Yucatecan restaurant.

típico *(TEE-pee-coe)* ADJECTIVE—This is a sign to stay away from. It's designed to attract you, the ethnocentric visitor, to spend your hard-earned foreign currency on things that you believe are the real deal. Pay no heed.

If you see it on a clothing store as in *ropa típica* or *trajes típicos*, it means that they sell clothing that the locals would not be seen dead in and only wear when obligated to do so for tourists, official government functions or school plays. If you buy and dare to wear this stuff you will look ridiculous, no matter how intensely you feel you are "blending in."

If you see a restaurant sign reading *comida típica*, it means that it is a place where no local would ever go. It also means that while the names of the *platillos* sound true, the only thing the restaurant really offers is a convenient location to a bus stop or a main square; the food will generally range in quality from bad to horrible. Stay away.

tirix ta' *(tee-reesh-TAH)* NOUN—Mayan for "diarreah." In many a Yucatecan household, no matter what socioeconomic group, this is the accepted and used term for what in English are called the runs. Note that I said household, so don't be pestering new acquaintances with your bathroom horror stories—some level of *confianza* must exist first.

tomar *(toh-MAHR)* VERB—Although literally it means "to take," this meaning is usurped by the more popular *agarrar (SEE agarrar)*. *Tomar* in Yucatan means "to drink;" in most cases anything such as coffee (*vamos tomar un cafecito*), soda, water; but more often than not, *tomar* is related to alcoholic beverages. When you are drinking in the local cantina, you are *tomando los tragos*. If you get home drunk, your partner/

wife/girlfriend might ask you accusingly:

▸ *¿Estuvistes tomando con tus amigos?*
Were you drinking with your buddies?

And continue this line of interrogation with:

▸ *Es que cada vez que sales con ese Juan, vienes a la casa tomado.*
Every time you go out with that Johnnie, you come home drunk.

tope *(TOH-pay)* NOUN—The average driver in Mexico will not read traffic signs, could care less about pedestrians and is always in more of a hurry than the people driving around him or her (his or her time is more important than that of the rest of the world). The police, in charge of driving in Yucatan as well whatever else that they do, practically give drivers licenses away and inspire no respect whatsoever from local drivers when directing them. The solution then, in the culture capital of the Americas, is to lay down strips of raised concrete to force drivers to slow down. These raised concrete automotive destructor units, are called *topes*, probably from the verb *topar* (con) or bump (into).

trago *(TRAH-go)* NOUN—An alcoholic drink.

▸ *¿Quieres un trago?*
Do you want a drink?

▸ *Vamos a tomar los tragos.*
Let's go drinking.

▸ *Se fue de tragos.*
He went on a binge.

trepar *(treh-PAHR)* UPWARDLY MOBILE VERB—To climb, as in a tree or a staircase. As the indication is that there is upward movement, *trepar* has permeated other similar ideas as well; I have heard it used in reference to increasing the volume of the music at a party. *Trépalo* (*TREH-pal-loh*) means "turn it up."

A most recent variation that I heard just the other day involved the ever-escalating prices of goods and services. "*Los precios siguen trepando*" I was told.

tuch *(TOOCH)* MAYAN NOUN—You will hear this a lot in the Yucatan; where no one in their right mind would call their bellybutton by its Castilian term, *ombligo*. Expressions using this word are many, including:

> *rascarse el tuch*
> scratching one's bellybutton—not do anything

> *el tuch del mundo*
> bellybutton of the world—center of the universe (romantic Yucatecans' (e.g. Fernando Espejo) idealized vision of Merida)

tun (*TOON*) MAYAN NOUN AND POPULAR SUFFIX—You will see the *tun* syllable at the end of names whilst driving across the Yucatan. The word means "rock" or "stone" and knowing this will help you figure out to some extent what the names of the towns mean. Some examples include:

> *Dzinitun*

> *Dzibilchaltun*

> *Xcanatun*

> *Hoctun*

> *Aktun Ha*

And many others.

tunkul (*toon-COOL*) PERCUSSIVE NOUN—For use in Mayan ceremonies, drums made from hollowed out logs, with horizontal openings on top. They were played with mallets wrapped in deerskins. They are often fancifully carved with Mayan motifs.

U

uay (*WHY, pronounced short and fast*) EXPRESSION OF SURPRISE, FEAR.—If you want to easily determine whether or not a person is truly Yucatecan, sneak up from behind and scare him—if he jumps and exclaims ¡UY! (*OOEE!*) then he is not from the peninsula. Probably a *wach* (SEE *wach*). But if he shouts ¡UAY! then you've got a real Yucatecan!

Also used when hearing a story about something amazing; for example, upon learning that Don Fulano was suddenly taken to the hospital and that it looks serious, a Yucatecan might remark

▸ *¿Uay, pues qué tiene el pobre?*
Gee whiz, what does the poor devil have?

UADY (*WHA-dee*) LEARNED NOUN—Interestingly, the word so associated with the Yucatecans, *uay*, consists of the initials of the local university, Universidad Autonoma de Yucatan as it should be abbreviated, but strangely is not. Someone has included a *D* in there to make it UADY.

Here's my own completely unproven theory on the subject: At some point in the university's history, someone who had obviously been laughed at when travelling to other parts of the country for his Yucatecan way of speaking, decided that it would be better if the university's name was not shortened to UAY, as this would be an open invitation for other universities to make fun of the Yucatecans yet again. This person decided to include the small word *de* which does not appear in any other university in Mexico. The UACH (Universidad Autonoma *de* Chapingo), UNAM (Universidad Nacional Autonoma *de* México) and others do not use the initial *D* in their shortened name. Only the UAY does, to make it UADY. ¡Uay!

ueputa also **jueputa** (*we-POO-tuh*) NOUN—Common on the street, the construction site and other places not really elegant, this is an abbreviated and less explicit form of saying *hijo de puta*, which literally means "son of a whore." The English equivalent would be "son of a bitch" and its contraction "sunuvabitch." If you were to do the scaring experiment mentioned in *uay*, a more down-to-earth person might exclaim "*Ueputa!*" My favorite anecdote involving this expression is the following:

Working in a restaurant in Cancun one late afternoon many moons ago, a hurricane just having passed, we were replacing the tables and chairs that had been stored for the duration of the storm, outside on the terrace. A lone elderly woman sat down to order her dinner. She was dressed conservatively and looked mild mannered enough. Suddenly, a strong gust of chilly wind ripped across the terrace and the lady jumped up and exclaimed in a loud voice, "*Jueputa!*" and quickly went for cover. So much for appearances!

Ueputa also refers to someone you don't care much for, a real jerk, someone who you can't stand. *Ese jueputa de Juan*. On construction sites and other workplaces, it's not uncommon to hear the supervisor yelling at some subordinate, "*Dale ueputa!*" which indicates that he wants the worker in question to pick up the pace a little.

universidad (*oo-nee-vehr-see-DAHD*)—A place of higher learning; Merida has several universities: the Autonoma de Yucatan (SEE *UADY*), the state's oldest and most respected post-high school learning center; the Universidad Autonoma de Chapingo, which, coming from the center of the country has the most appropriate initials: UACH; the Marista, featuring religion as a main course; and the preppy UniMayab or Universidad del Mayab.

This last one is the education center of choice for the more privileged kids from Merida whose parents wanted their kid to get a degree but also wanted them to stay near home. Why send them abroad anyway as it would only cause confusion and upset their acceptance of the way things are? Many parents believe that once you send your kids abroad, they come back as dope-smoking hippies who no longer accept the status quo in the formerly "White City."

So a group of local investors got together and formed their own university with a strong emphasis on good old-fashioned Catholic values and voila; a university was born. Many of Merida's so-called *clase acomodada* children go there to get their post-secondary education and if you are driving on the highway to Dzibilchaltún around 7 a.m., you may well find yourself being passed by Audis and BMWs along with other shiny new cars of lesser prestige.

The UniMayab is very popular with monied folks from neighbouring states such as Campeche and Tabasco, which don't have a "nice" university, so they send their children here to study among—and socialize with—kids of their socio-economic strata.

Uxmal (*oosh-MAHL*) MAYAN SITE—Probably the most beautiful site in the state of Yucatan in terms of the sheer number of restored buildings and the details of the constructions. Thanks to the fact that it is located in an area not known for its *cenotes* or any other water source, it was not dismantled by the invading Spanish to build their churches, streets or mansions, and Uxmal remained untouched and largely intact. If you were to visit just one Mayan site in your time in the Yucatan, this must be it.

V

v (*veh*, also *beh*)—Twenty-second letter of the English alphabet, its ambivalent pronunciation (SEE *b*), makes it a useful letter for confusing and amusing results in spelling throughout the country. Valet becomes *balet; viaje, biaje; vamos, bamos* etc. etc.

v (*veh*)—There is an interesting, and very Yucatecan use for the letter *v*. It is not a conscious use of the *v*; but rather, a pronunciation thing. It goes something like this. There is a category of Yucatecans, who, through assimilation, vocal laziness or, as some say, pretentiousness, can not pronounce the double *r* so necessary in Spanish pronunciation. The double *r* as you know appears in many words like *garrapata, agarrar* and others, and is also used when a word begins with *r* such as *Rafael, razonable,* and *rápido*. The pronunciation is a very soft *v*, almost French in its sound (hence the accusations of pretentiousness). See what happens to the word when it is pronounced by one of these linguistically challenged persons:

- *Garrapata*
  Gavapata

- *Agarrar*
  Agavar

- *Rafael*
  Vafael

- *Razonable*
  Vazonable

- *Rápido*
  Vápido

valet parking (*hey, this one's easy*)—This term lifted from the English has survived the non-existent translation almost unscathed. I say almost, because from time to time it will be spelled *balet,* which sounds pretty artsy fartsy to me, and occasionally you will see that Valet Parking is not only an activity where a person parks someone else's vehicle, but also a job description. As in:

> *Se solicita un Valet Parking*
> Valet Parking Wanted (the business places the ad and is looking for a guy to drive cars)

> *Soy el valet parking.*
> I am the valet parking.

viaje (*vee-YA-hey*) TRAVELLING NOUN—The term used to describe any trip to another place; e.g. *viaje de compras a Houston* and *viaje de placer o de negocios a Miami*. Also used in a very Yucatecan way by the service personnel—maids, gardeners, etc.—when they go home for the weekend, as in *voy a viajar,* when they return to their *pueblos* outside Merida. Used by many Yucatecans to describe their pilgrimage to such exotic destinations as Ticul or Progreso, which are considered far enough away to be called *viajes*. Often used in this context in conjunction with *voy a agarrar carretera*. Literally: I'm going to grab/take the highway.

video (*vih-DAY-oh*) NOUN—Not so long ago, in the Yucatan, you were nobody if you didn't have one of these, and it's not a home movie of your kids visiting the Centenario we're talking about. It was the VCR, or video cassette recorder, and every self-respecting household had one. Calling it a VCR was too complicated, and *videocasetera* too long, so it was just called *el video*. The ubiquitous *video* has been replaced by the *debedé*. The name *video* is still used for a store specializing in the rental and sale of movies, no longer as video cassettes but rather DVDs.

vuelta (*v-WELL-tah*) NOUN—A spin. If you are driving along with no particular destination in mind and ask someone to come along you would ask them to come along for a spin or *una vuelta*. People also spin in places such as shopping malls. While you dip into a store to check out the latest offerings on the sale rack, your friend might say to you: "*Voy a estar aquí, dando vueltas.*" He or she will walking around while they wait, but literally, the phrase means "I will be here, spinning around on my axis." I always hope they don't get dizzy and fall over.

W

wach (*watch*) HEAVY NOUN—An entire chapter could be written about *waches* in the Yucatan, where this classification was once applied to anyone who came from someplace beyond Campeche. Now it is used almost exclusively for those from Mexico City and environs. Also known in other parts of *la república* as *chilangos*, a *wach* can be identified by his accent, his dress, and never-ending struggle to climb that elusive social ladder. There are of course many wonderful, kind, generous and well-mannered *waches*. It's just that some of them conform so well to a negative stereotype that they they tarnish the reputations of the better examples that do exist. *Wach* is a derogative term, used in whispers at Yucatecan ladies coffee sessions, and comes from the Mayan language. The word's origins are said to come from the time of Salvador Alvarados march through the Yucatan with his sandal-wearing central Mexican troops. The sound of those sandals slapping against feet and stone apparently gave their wearers the name that sticks to this day.

wachada (*watch-ADA*) NOUN—Any silly, corny or ridiculous thing that only a *wach* would do. For example, if you are a man, wear black socks almost to your knees along with shorts and sandals when at the beach. The word illustrates again the ingenious merging of the Spanish suffix (*ada*) and Mayan root word (*wach*).

wah' (*WHA*) NOUN—This is one of those Mayan words that really doesn't have even a Spanish translation. It is said that some people are born with a purplish blotch called a *wah'* on their skin (also known as a Mongolian spot) usually on their thorax somewhere and when these people get upset, this blotch becomes a little brighter or more pronounced. Hence the term *retentado el wah'* for when someone gets angry. (SEE *retentado*)

way (SEE *Uay*)

wixar (*wi-SHAHR*) VERB—In Mayan/Spanish, to urinate. *Uix* is the Mayan part, the *ar* suffix is from the Spanish. The *W* is added in place of the *U* to ensure correct pronunciation and make it look more "normal." I have had lengthy discussions with Yucatecans who insist that *wach* is spelled *huach* but that have no qualms about the spelling of *wixando*. Since Mayan is an ancient language and I am pretty sure the current alphabet was not in use at the time of their predominance in the region, we can safely assume that you can spell *wach, wech,* and *wix* pretty well any darn way you want.

Now, back to the word. If you really have to go pee and are among close friends who won't be offended if you reveal your most basic physiological necessities, you might tell them *"me estoy wixando,"* which literally means, I'm peeing my pants. *Wixar* is like a regular *ar* verb, and be conjugated normally. For example:

▶▶ *yo wixo*

▶▶ *tú wixas*

▶▶ *el/ella wixa*

▶▶ *nosotros wixamos*

▶▶ *ustedes wixan*

▶▶ *ellos/ellas wixan*

You know how in those movies where the stern teacher prohibits the little native Indian kid from speaking his language and makes him speak English? This used to happen in some remote corners of the Yucatan where teachers insisted that the kids not use the term *wixar*, telling them that it was wrong and, in some cases, even a bad word.

On a more personal note, we use this word in our family when travelling in areas where Mayan is not spoken. If one member of the family needs to go to the bathroom and she doesn't want to announce it to the world around her, she will tell us, "I'm going to make a wish," and we know exactly that we need to stop for a bathroom break. Of course, using the Mayan term in an English context like this makes such popular expressions as "when you wish upon a star."

wixóm (*wi-SHOM*) NOUN—A crossbred Mayan/Spanish expression that refers to teenagers or young adults in a derogatory or belittling sort of way; e.g. *"esos wixones 'tan haciendo MUCHO escandalo"* (those young kids are really raising a ruckus). From the Mayan *wix* or *uix* (pee, as in urinate—SEE *above*) and modified by the Spanish *on* suffix.

X

x 1) (*EH-keess*)—In Merida and all of the Yucatan, the *x* is pronounced *sh*; this is a Mayan thing. You can always tell when someone is a nasty *wach* when they say they took their relatives to the ruins of *Ooksmal*, when they really should be saying *Ooshmal*. Avoid this common *faux pas* and you won't be mistaken for a *wach* or ignorant foreigner.

2) (*EH-keess*)—When writing the 2010 edition of this dictionary, Mexican youth used this letter as an expression of indifference. If they find something uninteresting (during those difficult teen years everything is boring) or are too lazy to communicate verbally, they will answer *x* to any number of queries, ranging from "How was the movie/party/class?" to "Are you sure you want to wear that?" to which the appropriate answer is *"ay 'X' mamá."*

3) (*SH*)—In the Mayan language, inserting the *SH* sound in front of a word makes it *despectivo* or turns the affected word into an object of contempt. *Bolsa* (purse) becomes *x'la bolsa*, for example if the purse you are commenting on is contempt-worthy.

xcam (*SHCAHM*) NOUN—From Xcan, the name of a town in Yucatan, and yet another popular term for a male homosexual. In conservative, Catholic Merida, it is amazing how many words there are for these apparently deviant sexual orientations! The term apparently comes from the fact that the town of Xcan, located on the border between the states of Yucatan and Quintana Roo, has never defined its geographic situation politically speaking. This lack of definition is therefore applied to anyone displaying homosexual tendencies.

> *¿Conoces a Pedro?*
> Do you know Pedro?

> *¡Sí hombre! Treeeeeeeemendo x'can!*
> Sure do! What a queer!

xic (SHEEK) NOUN—Part of the human anatomy, namely the armpit. No one in their right Yucatecan mind would ever call their armpit an *axila*, which is the Spanish term for it; everyone, this foreigner included, uses the Mayan term *xic*. It's so much more poetic, easier on the tongue and versatile. For example:

If someone walks by and you can smell his or her body odor, you might be inspired to exclaim to the person next to you, providing you know him or her and have their *confianza*, "¡Uay! Me dió un xicazo," which means literally that you got a whiff of *xic* blown your way from the offending person. By the way, if you smell something strongly reminiscent of *xic* and you see no one is around, there are two options: a) you need a shower, or b) there is a hot dog cart on the corner (clue: it's the onions).

xic

xix (SHEESH) NOUN—Another incorporation of precise, one-syllable Mayan words into everyday Yucatecan Spanish. Technically, the *xix* is the sediment left when a liquid has been consumed. In the neighbouring state of Tabasco, a traditional drink called *pozol* is made with cocoa and corn, ground up and mixed with water. This is drunk and the sediment that inevitably gets left on the bottom is called the *shish*. The Tabasqueños have a problem with the whole *x=sh* thing and write their *xix*, *shish*.

Nowadays, the *xix* is what is left at the bottom of the bottle of Coke when you have practically finished it. The *xix* is what's in your gas tank when you barely make to the gas station before having the car stall. *El xix* is what's left when everyone has had their fill of the *frijol con puerco* and there's just a little bit of broth in the pot.

▶▶ *¿Quieres un poco? Nada mas queda un xix.*
Want some? There's only a little bit left.
(Don't get your hopes up.)

The term *xix* is now also applied to those last moments of the party when practically everyone has gone home and you are with one or two people, criticizing happily all those who have left before and the stupid things they said and did. *El xix de la fiesta*.

This word is extremely popular—use it and be loved by the Yucatecans as one of their own.

Xmatkuil (*shmaht-QUEEL*) PLACE—Xmatkuil is a suburb (OK, a small village very close to Merida) that is unremarkable except that every year the state holds its annual fair there. This is a popular event, as in the definition of the word *popular* in this very dictionary you are now holding in your hands. Highlights include cock fights; midnight concerts by mostly has-been Mexican bands and musical artists who can no longer fill an arena and spend their time shuttling from state fair to state fair; livestock exhibits; thrilling rides on precariously installed machinery; many a sad clown, and shows by transvestites swearing at each other at full volume. Something for everyone!

Did I mention the infamous and *chot-nak*-inducing food stands offering hot dog wieners and plantain or potato chips, all deep fried? The wieners are particularly interesting as each wiener is cut into thirds and the ends cut partially lengthwise, when the pieces are tossed into the hot fat the ends appetizingly curl up. These items are served with the cheapest possible watery ketchup on the market.

Should you find yourself in Merida in November, a visit to Xmatkuil is a must to experience for yourself the sights, aromas, and sounds of this traditional event.

Y

y Almost the last letter of the alphabet. Like the letter *j*, always mispronounced. While the *j* becomes a *y* (*Yanet, Yon Secada*, etc.), the letter *y* becomes a *j*. The other day I was listening to a sports correspondent on the radio mention the *New Jork Jankees*. It's not like they can't say the letter *y*; they do it whenever there is a *j* for crying out loud. So what is it?

yach (*YUCH*) MAYAN VERB—Meaning to squish or press, most commonly with the fingers, some kind of soft pulpy mass, until the material oozes out between your fingers. It is used combined with Spanish as in *hacerle yach* to whatever it is you are squishing.

yaya (*YAH-yah*) NOUN—An "ouch." (SEE *lastimada*)

Yuca (*YOO-kah*) NOUN—A Yucatecan. Male or female, this is what Yucatecans sometimes call themselves. "*Somos Yucas*," they'll say with pride if they're asked in a restaurant in Campeche where they're from (if there was at all any doubt).

YucaWach (*YOO-kah-watch* or *yoo-ka-WATCH*) NOUN—A variety of possible situations warrant the application of this term. Extensive research has unearthed the following:

1) A person born in the nations' capital who moved to and lives in Merida since a very early age.

2) A Yucatecan, born in Merida, who moved to Mexico City and grew up there, only to find the gravitational pull of his *tierra* so irresistible that he has returned to find himself in the unenviable position of not quite fitting in anymore.

3) A Yucatecan, obviously so by his appearance, acting loud and obnoxious, like a *wach*, hence the term.

Z

zacate (*sah-CAH-teh*—rhymes with *Tecate*, the beer) NOUN—OK, this was a stretch but something had to be included for the letter *z*, so often confused with the *s* and the *c*. *Zacate* is the term used locally for grass or lawn, as opposed to *cesped*, heard in other parts of the country. (SEE ALSO *pasto*)

zaguán (*sah-GWUM*) NOUN—The foyer or entranceway to your home, usually occupied by a couple of potted plants and maybe a crucifix. These are found only in larger homes, as the popular classes haven't got the space in their homes for one of these.

zampar (*sahm-PAHR*) VERB—To fill oneself up (with food); to eat. Its usage is common but it is still an unusual word in that you won't learn it in your Spanish class. Its meaning in the local context is exactly as defined by the very official *Diccionario Kapelusz*. You can use it like this:

> ▶ *Me zampé unos tacos.*
> I wolfed down some *tacos*.

> ▶ *¿Te zampaste todo el pastel?*
> Did you eat all that cake?

Zeta (*ZEH-tah*) NOUN—While *Zeta* is what the last letter of the alphabet is called, it is also the name of a violent drug gang operating in Mexico, especially in the southeast. So while this is not in itself a Yucatecan term, you will hear it mentioned in your conversations with locals, unfortunately, at the time of this writing.

Made in the USA
Lexington, KY
01 October 2013